Dear Hillary,

I hope this book brings back memories of Singapore for you.

All the Best,

Wan Cheng,

PASTEL PORTRAITS

1984
Published by the Singapore Coordinating Committee
Produced by the PASTEL PORTRAITS Editorial Committee
Designed by Viscom Design Associates
Typesetting by Superskill Services
Colour separation by Scantrans Pte Ltd.

Text by Gretchen Liu
Photographs by R. Ian Lloyd and Ian C. Stewart
by Kuou Shang-Wei: pages 44, 57, 58, 74 (bottom), 75 (bottom),
76 (bottom), 77 (top), 102, 103, 127, 131, 142, 143, 144, 145
from the National Museum, Singapore: pages 22, 27, 37, 43, 139 and 146
by Concept Media: page 103
by Henry Wong for Interior Digest: page 105.

Acknowledged:
The National Museum, Singapore: maps on pages 13 and 15.
The National Archives and Oral History Department, Singapore:
building plans on pages 20, 21, 147 and 148.

Fifth Impression 1992
Print consultancy by Wordmaker Design Pte Ltd
Printed by Welpac Printing & Packaging Pte Ltd
Colour separation by Singapore Sang Choy.

Sole Distributor:
Select Books
19 Tanglin Road #03-15
Tanglin Shopping Centre
Singapore 1024

ISBN 9971-88-020-2

PASTEL PORTRAITS

SINGAPORE'S ARCHITECTURAL HERITAGE

Text by Gretchen Liu
Photographs by R. Ian Lloyd, Ian C. Stewart and Kuou Shang-Wei
Designed by Viscom Design Associates

Published by the Singapore Coordinating Committee
Goh Hup Chor, William S.W. Lim, Kenneth Chen, Seah Kim Bee and Tan Teck Min

R. IAN LLOYD

FOREWORD

The history of a city is recorded not only in books, but also in its buildings. While the written word captures the evolution of events and beliefs, buildings embody lifestyles and aesthetic tastes, technology and crafts. Therefore old buildings are more than just bricks and mortar. Old town houses and shops, temples and churches, schools and institutions, are more than utilitarian objects. They also are a record of our ancestors' aspirations and achievements. In Singapore, many of the old buildings embody the visual confluence of our multi-varied ethnic roots. While the majority need some face-lift, they never cease to delight our eyes and enhance the sense of time and place unique to our own city.

I am delighted to see that exactly a quarter century after self-Government, a group of our citizens, both professionals and businessmen, got together to produce this beautiful visual record of our historic buildings and districts. We must realise that photographs and words are no substitute for life-size forms and spaces. For one cannot walk into or around the buildings in these photographs. Meanwhile ageing artisans and their crafts vanish with the passage of time. Buildings demolished are history records gone. While some must make way for progress, some, we hope, will remain to link us with our past.

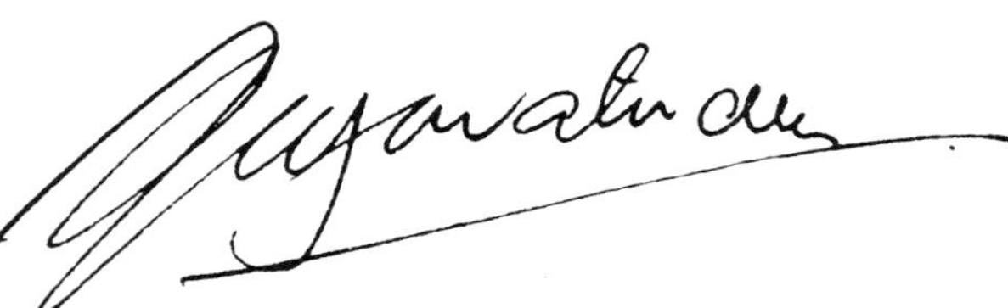

S. Rajaratnam

Second Deputy Prime Minister (Foreign Affairs)

ACKNOWLEDGEMENTS

PASTEL PORTRAITS owes its conception to the members of the Singapore Coordinating Committee. The committee, formed in mid-1983 to plan an international seminar on Adaptive Re-Use of Old Buildings held in Singapore April 28 to May 2, 1984, decided that the seminar provided a perfect opportunity to produce a record of Singapore's architectural heritage. The committee included Goh Hup Chor (Chairman), an architect and urban designer; William S.W. Lim (Secretary), an architect; Kenneth Chen, an architect; Seah Kim Bee, a chartered town planner; and Tan Teck Min, a planner.

The next step was to form an editorial committee to translate the raw concept into photographs and words. For those of us on the committee, PASTEL PORTRAITS became a voyage of discovery as we walked city streets and discovered just how remarkably rich and eclectic Singapore is in historic architecture. Committee chairman William S.W. Lim organised many meetings held to discuss the project and nurtured it through the various stages. Writer M. Gretchen, a journalist with The Straits Times, worked closely with graphic designer Ko Hui Huy of Viscom Design Associates as they fit together text, photographs, historical references and maps. The job was not unlike the assemblage of a complicated jig saw puzzle. Evelyn Lip, Senior Lecturer in the School of Architecture at the National University of Singapore, provided the initial research material.

Jane Perkins, an editor with The Times Organisation, gave creative support, proofread and helped with last minute cross-checking. Tan Teck Min, an urban planner, provided guidance and suggestions during the early stages. Mok Wei Wei, an architect, also helped with last minute cross-checking. Lu Guang Chi, manager (Culture/Education and Development) at Lianhe Zaobao/Wanbao coordinated the Chinese translation.

The three photographers involved in PASTEL PORTRAITS patiently captured streetscapes, facades and details. R. Ian Lloyd, Ian Charles Stewart and Kuou Shang-wei discovered, like the rest of us, the breadth of Singapore's architectural heritage.

Many other individuals gave assistance to PASTEL PORTRAITS. George Bogaars, Seow Eu Jin, Liu Thai Ker, Goh Hup Chor and Arun Mahizhnan read the early draft of the Introduction and made useful comments. Jane Ferguson also read an early draft of the manuscript and pointed out several inconsistencies. A special thanks goes to Peter Keys who graciously gave assistance in captioning, proofreading and for kindly providing the material for the Glossary. John Logan also proofread.

Librarians at many institutions gave cheerful assistance. We would like to thank the librarians and staff at the National Museum, the National Archives and Oral History Department and the National Library for help in both picture and text research. We also take the opportunity here to thank them for allowing us to reproduce maps, old photographs and building plans on the pages that follow. We also wish to thank the librarians at the National University of Singapore Library, The Straits Times Library and the Bukit Merah Library. A number of students from the School of Architecture helped gather research materials. They include Low Heng Huat, Gwee Boon Chuan, Lena Quek, Teo Yeow Khoon, Wong Hong Meng, Kwok Ying Yao and Choo Heok Jiang.

Our graphic designers frequently and patiently reworked layouts as we refined our thinking. Sylvia S.H. Tan, Ko Hui Huy, Molly Sung, Annie Tan and Peggy Lim of Viscom Design Associates became intimately involved with the book's evolution.

Thanks must also be given to Julie Hui, secretary of the editorial committee, and Florence Tan who typed the manuscript.

Finally, PASTEL PORTRAITS would not have been possible without the generous support of our sponsors, Mobil Oil Singapore Pte Ltd as well as Reliance Contractors Pte Ltd; Metrobilt Construction Pte Ltd; The Times Organisation; Lee Kim Tah (Pte) Ltd; Progressive Builders Pte Ltd and Singapore Piling & Civil Engineering Pte Ltd. Nan Yang Xing Zhou Lianhe Zaobao provided funds for the Chinese translation of PASTEL PORTRAITS.

CONTENTS

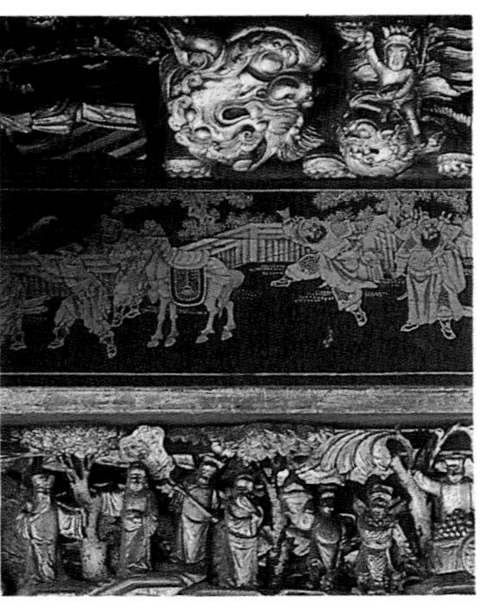

PREFACE TO THE FOURTH IMPRESSION

PASTEL PORTRAITS captures a moment of time in an ever-changing cityscape. First published in April of 1984, the book was launched at the opening of an international seminar on the adaptive reuse of old buildings. It was conceived as a seductive record of the richness and beauty of Singapore's architectural heritage. No one expected the first edition to sell out, much less a fourth impression to appear six years later.

The intervening years have seen many changes to the urban landscape, some of them happily related to the conservation of the buildings and districts captured on the pages of this book. Take, for example, the photograph of South Boat Quay on page 28. Absent is Singapore's current tallest building, OUB Centre, which at that time was just a hole in the ground. The familiar shophouses which line the river, however, still cling firmly to the river bank and look much as they did when the photograph was taken in 1984. They will be spruced up over the next few years as they are now part of the Boat Quay Conservation Area.

Boat Quay is one of the 10 Conservation Areas gazetted by the government in 1989, the same year that the Urban Redevelopment Authority was formally made the Conservation Authority. The other areas are Bukit Pasoh, Cairnhill, Clarke Quay, Emerald Hill, Kampong Glam, Kreta Ayer, Little India, Tanjong Pagar and Telok Ayer. While the names and boundaries of these areas do not precisely coincide with the chapters in this book, all are represented. Tanjong Pagar and Bukit Pasoh, for example, appear in the Neil Road chapter on pages 51 to 56.

Within these areas are hundreds of pre-World War Two buildings, many of them shophouses and residential terrace houses which date from circa 1870 to the 1930s. While by no means unique to Singapore, these building forms have been crucial to the shaping of the city's character. Today, it is the contrast between the intimate scale and ornate details of these mainly two, three and four-storey buildings, on the one hand, and the clean lines and massive scale of modern developments, on the other, that creates a uniquely Singaporean city.

As we wrote in the Preface to the first edition of PASTEL PORTRAITS the city did not come about easily. Its character was formed by countless skilled and unskilled workers, hundreds of professionals, and generations of individual decision-makers who responded to the building fashions of the time and utilized the technology and materials available to them. The nation's multi-ethnic roots are discernable in this record. Malay, Chinese, Indian and Classical European traditions converged here and expressed themselves in the common medium of brick, plaster, timber and glazed tiles.

Fortunately the results of some conservation projects are already visible. In Tanjong Pagar, for example, a pilot conservation project feasibility study carried out by the Urban Redevelopment Authority in 1985 led to the restoration of 32 shophouse units in the area. The remaining 196 shophouses were tendered out and are being restored by the private sector. While many have temporarily lost that attractive patina of age, their rotting timbers, leaking roofs and flaking plaster have been properly repaired. With time, the colours will soften and the patina return. Emerald Hill, with its close proximity to Orchard Road, is once again a desirable residential area. Many of the terrace houses along the curved, inclined road have now been renovated in a manner sympathetic to their age and character while the road itself has been landscaped. The result is charming.

Equally important is the conservation of individual buildings or smaller groupings. Empress Place, a mid-19th century colonial building on the north bank of the Singapore River, has already become an elegant exhibition venue. The old police barracks at Hill Street is now the National Archives while on Fort Canning, an old British Army building is being turned into a permanent home for a ballet and a theatre group. The Raffles Hotel, designated a national monument in 1887, is presently undergoing a massive restoration due for completion in 1991 that will see it once again become a grand hotel of the East. The Victorian cast-iron Telok Ayer Market in the heart of the business district has also been restored and will have a new lease of like as a festival marketplace. At Clarke Quay, the entire area of godowns and shophouses will be restored and turned into a festival marketplace by 1993.

Among the buildings also earmarked for conservation are those in the grounds of the Convent of the Holy Infant Jesus as well as St Joseph's School. Along Stamford Road, the variety of building styles seen on pages 76 to 79 will also remain part of the city for many years to come. Many of these buildings will see their uses change after restoration. Equally important are attempts to integrate restored and new structures within a single redevelopment project. Conservation efforts are not limited to the central area. Shophouses and other individual buildings scattered around the island may be added to the conservation list. Clearly there is much work ahead.

Thus Singapore has embarked on a conservation programme with the same vigour displayed in earlier urban development efforts. The housing shortage faced on self-rule three decades ago has been eradicated, an ultra-modern skyline faces the sea and the reclaimed land of Marina South and Marina Centre await an entire new city. Fortunately, despite the speed of urban renewal, many old areas remained undisturbed in the 1980s and are now being restored to complement new projects. When all the development plans currently on the drawing board are fully realised, Singapore will be a tropical city of excellence. One of its components will certainly be a treasured and well-kept architectural heritage.

PASTEL PORTRAITS records only a portion of Singapore's old buildings. Many fine examples could not be included in the limited number of pages. While the camera reveals the subtle variations and beauty of handcrafted details, it could not capture the intimate scale nor quality of the streets. These, however, can be experienced by future generations for themselves.

Gretchen Liu
1990

INTRODUCTION

The founding of modern Singapore was a fortuitous meeting of geography and history.

The island provided a good harbour at a position of prominence along the Straits of Malacca at the crossroads of trade between the Indian Ocean, and the Pacific Ocean and the South China Sea. It was the choice of Sir Stamford Raffles, an agent of the East India Company. He was looking for a port at the southern tip of the Malay Peninsula along the Straits to add to the company's settlements at Bencoolen, on Sumatra's western coast, and Penang to complete British dominance of this important waterway and to advantageously compete with the Dutch strongholds at Batavia and Malacca.

Raffles landed on the shore of the Singapore River and signed a treaty with the local chieftain, Temenggong Abdu'r Rahman of Johor, on 30 January, 1819. The treaty granted a strip of land along the coast for an outpost. At the time there were about 40 Chinese gambier plantations, 150 Malay *orang laut* (pirates) and about one hundred houses clustered around the river mouth dominated by the house of the Temenggong. Almost within hours of Raffles' landing, the placid calm was swept away as he ordered work on the new settlement. Some reports say that redevelopment started the very next day. Within a short while, the settlement looked like a temporary toehold of commercialism over which the jungle might again prevail.

Success and growth came quickly, thanks to Singapore's convenient location, Raffles' free trade policy and the settlement's comparative orderliness. By 1820, the swampy south bank of the river was covered with Chinese houses and the Bugis Village in Kampong Glam was an extensive town. In the first two and a half years the number of ships and boats calling at Singapore totalled nearly 3,000. By 1821, the population was 5,000, including many Nanyang Chinese from other parts of the region, and five miles of roads had been laid. By 1823 the first bridge, market and a residence for the officer-in-charge had been built. By 1824, when

The Town Plan

"The revised town plan involved a large-scale resettlement of the existing population, and to help him Raffles appointed a committee in November 1822 consisting of one European merchant and two officials, who were to consult representatives of the Malay, Chinese, Bugis, Javanese and Arab communities.
Financial compensation and free land were offered to people who were forced to move from their houses and the old bazaar but the upheaval caused considerable trouble and inconvenience, and the police had to be called in to evict residents and pull down buildings. The days of haphazard building were at an end."

– *C.M. Turnbull, A History of Singapore 1819-1975.*

the East India Company signed a second treaty with the Sultan, which handed over the whole island to the British, the population had shot up to 11,000 and the city was developing a slightly more permanent character.

Raffles visited Singapore on only three occasions. On his brief second visit in May 1819 he was accompanied by immigrants from Penang including the versatile Naraini Pillai. Pillai became, among other things, the first building contractor on record, and was responsible for the founding of Sri Mariamman Temple on South Bridge Road – Singapore's first Hindu temple. In the hull of the ship *Indiana*, which carried the new arrivals, there was also a welcome supply of building materials.

On Raffles' third, longest and final visit he initiated the now famous Town Plan and set up a committee to oversee its implementation. Thus Singapore was a planned city almost from the start and the imprint of that plan can still be seen in the heart of the city today.

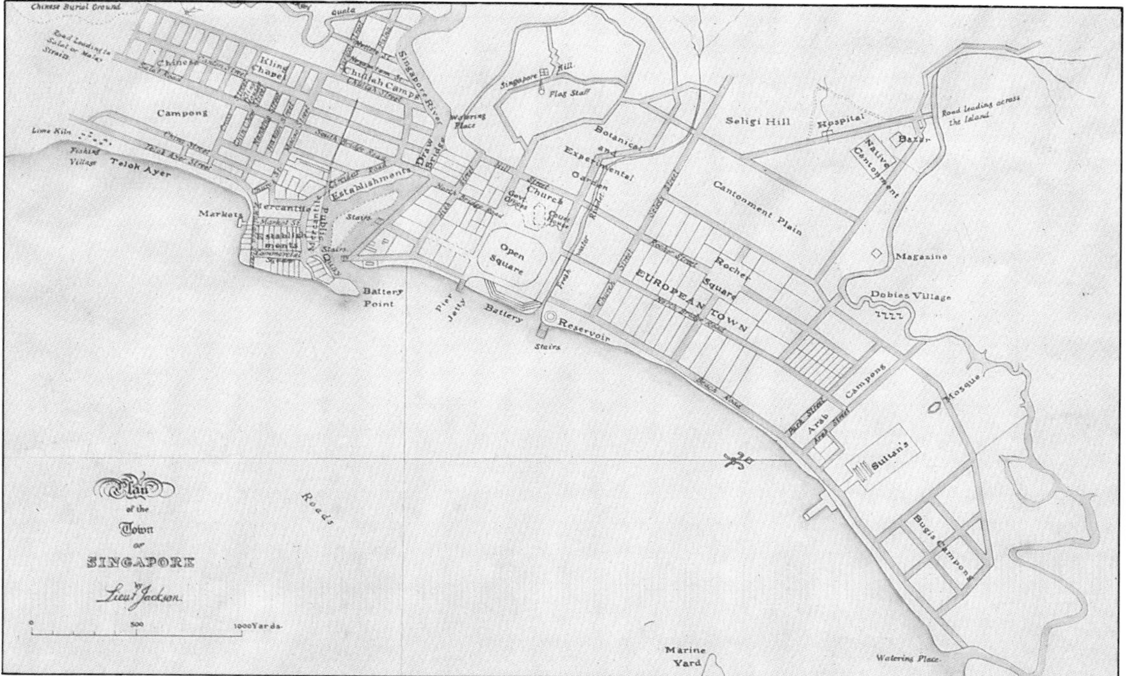

This "Plan of the Town of Singapore by Lieut. Jackson" was published in John Crawfurd's "Journal of an Embassy to the Courts of Siam and Cochin-China" in London in 1828. Initially accepted as an actual plan of the town as it existed in 1827, the map's authenticity was later questioned. Lieut. Jackson, a military engineer detailed by Raffles to assist the Town Planning Committee, probably drew it up in December 1822 or January 1823 to represent Raffle's idealistic vision — a vision which did not fully materialise. Scholars have not only pointed out various inaccuracies but also noted that the plan appears less like a survey than a planner's dream!

Raffles had arrived for his last visit on 10 October, 1822 after a three year absence. He found that the busy settlement had grown into a veritable jungle of disorderly buildings quite different from the city he had envisaged. He acted quickly. Within weeks the committee was appointed and on 4 November Raffles issued a set of guidelines, the Town Plan, to the members. The plan set aside the area directly north of the Singapore River for the use of government. The business area, which had already sprung up on this shore, was moved to the south bank, which was a swampy area occupied by Chinese living in tumbledown huts on stilts. So Raffles ordered these settlers to move out and had the bank filled with earth taken from a nearby hillock, thus creating both solid ground for South Boat Quay and a flat Commercial Square, or Raffles Place as it is now called.

To lessen the chances of inter-ethnic strife, separate kampongs and residential areas were set up for the various ethnic groups. Although the perimeters of these enclaves altered in time due to the pressures of an ever-expanding population, each group has retained an unchallenged claim to the areas allocated to them for most of Singapore's history.

The Chinese, who Raffles anticipated would always make up the largest single group, were given the whole of the area south of the river beyond Boat Quay and Commercial Square. Chinatown itself was divided into separate areas for the different dialect speaking groups. The Indians (Chulias) were moved to the Chulia Kampong on the south bank of the river further upsteam from Boat Quay at Chulia and Market Streets. The Europeans and rich Asians were given residential land to the north-east of the government area where Beach Road and North Bridge Road were laid out. And to the north-east of the European town was Kampong Glam where the followers of Sultan Hussein moved and where Arabs, Bugis and other Muslims were encouraged to settle. The Temenggong and his sprawling village of 600 followers at the mouth of the Singapore River were moved west of the town along the coast between Tanjong Pagar and Telok Blangah.

The plan also provided for a network of roads, for streets to be built "at right angles" and for the subdivision of land into lots and public spaces. A linear arrangement of shophouses of specified widths linked by a covered passageway was introduced "for the sake of regularity and conformity". All commercial buildings were to be constructed of masonry with tile roofs, while prosperous Asians and Europeans were encouraged to trade side by side. Sometime in early 1823 a regulation was passed creating a registry of land which sold plots on permanent lease by auction. By the time Raffles left Singapore in June, 1823 he was satisfied that the city would expand in an orderly manner.

Raffles spent less than a total of ten months in Singapore yet his achievements overshadow the considerable contributions of the first two British Residents. The first was William Farquhar, a popular, easy-going yet pragmatic administrator with years of experience in Malacca under his belt who had to cope with a shortage of staff, little money and the difficulty of communications. Between 1819 and 1823 the settlement prospered under his administration and thanks to him we have the Padang, or Esplanade as it was long known. Unfortunately, Farquhar clashed bitterly with the idealistic Raffles over certain policies and he was replaced by John Crawfurd. Between 1823 and 1826, this shrewd, formidable man, with the reputation of being tight-fisted, guided the growth of the city. Crawfurd was conscientious and painstaking but inspired little affection. But it was largely due to the abilities of both men that Raffles' vision of Singapore becoming "the pride and Emporium of the East" began to be realised.

Cities reveal as much about time as about place and the immediate post-Raffles period was one of quickly constructed, temporary buildings. The indefatigable diarist of the early years, Raffles's translator Munshi Abdullah, recorded: "Although the population was so large, there was not yet a single house built of

G.D. Coleman

"Mr Coleman, for many years, was employed under the Government as Superintendent of Convicts and Public Works, and to his good judgement and untiring energy we mainly owe the great extent of good roads on this island, and to his taste and skill as an architect we are also indebted for many of the elegant buildings, both public and private, which adorn Singapore. In June, 1841, he embarked for his native country, and after visiting all that is interesting in Europe, he had but recently returned here, with a view to a permanent residence, when he fell a prey to fever, brought on by exposure to the sun."

– *The Singapore Free Press (1844).*

The 1840s

"Improvements in town also proceed apace. Many – or we may say with truth, most – of the old wooden houses which in the beginning of the year gave such a ruinous and decaying look to the town, have now been replaced by handsome and substantial looking brick houses, and, ere many months more have passed, the principal streets bid fair to shew nothing but brick edifices, confining the wooden erections to the poorer parts of the town."

– An account written at the end of 1845 as quoted in An Anecdotal History of Old Times in Singapore 1819-1865 by C.B. Buckley.

stone. Their houses are all built of attap." Development centred on the south side of the town while the godowns vacated by the European merchants on the north bank of the river were used as government offices. Even the house of the Resident on Government Hill was a temporary-looking wood and attap affair.

During Raffles' final visit another man was in Singapore who was destined to play a crucial role in shaping the city's early skyline: George Drumgoole Coleman. Coleman, an architect, acted as consultant to Raffles on the 1822-23 Town Plan and seeing, no doubt, the tremendous potential in the new settlement for his practice, he moved to Singapore in 1826 from Batavia where he had worked for several years.

Ostensibly the 31-year-old talented Irishman came to take up the post of Town Surveyor but he was soon combining his official duties with a lucrative private practice. He designed many important buildings including a few which have withstood the test of time: The small, elegant Armenian Church (1835), the Caldwell House on the grounds of the Town Convent (1840), and the stately Maxwell House, for a Java merchant named John Argyle Maxwell (1826) which, in an enlarged, modified state is now Parliament House.

Within three years of his arrival Coleman built his own fine house along the street which today bears his name. It was demolished in 1969 to make way for the Peninsula Hotel and Shopping Centre. In 1833 Coleman became Superintendent of Public Works and he was the first Overseer of Convicts. In addition to his architectural contribution he did much to improve the town's infrastructure, overseeing the draining of marshes, the construction of roads and other public works.

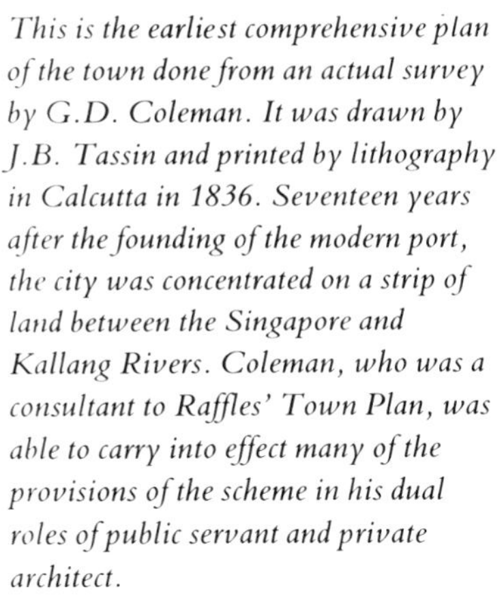

This is the earliest comprehensive plan of the town done from an actual survey by G.D. Coleman. It was drawn by J.B. Tassin and printed by lithography in Calcutta in 1836. Seventeen years after the founding of the modern port, the city was concentrated on a strip of land between the Singapore and Kallang Rivers. Coleman, who was a consultant to Raffles' Town Plan, was able to carry into effect many of the provisions of the scheme in his dual roles of public servant and private architect.

The style which Coleman brought with him to this soil was Palladian, the recognised idiom and established formal architectural style of 18th century England. It was carried overseas by architects until it penetrated the remotest colonies. The name Palladian is derived from the architecture of Andre Palladio (1518-80), a Venetian High Renaissance architect who was one of several architects who revived and reinterpreted the use of Greek and Roman Classical orders after an abeyance of a thousand years. From Italy the use of Classical orders travelled to England via wealthy Englishmen who did the Grand Tour of Europe and proceeded to imitate Palladian's style in their country houses. The Palladian tradition was imported into Singapore via the East India Company centres of government in Bombay and Calcutta, where the young Coleman had practised for several years building houses for merchants before moving further east to Batavia.

Coleman's genius lay in skilfully adapting the Palladian manner to suit the tropical climate. Well-versed in Classical proportions and symmetry, he combined Doric and Corinthian orders of architecture with elegant plasterwork and deep, wide verandahs, high ceilings, roof overhangs for shade, an open floor plan and louvred windows which gave light yet reduced glare. A high standard of design and craftsmanship developed under Coleman's influence which persisted long after his death in 1844.

Coleman was succeeded by a large number of anonymous builders and craftsmen, as well as a handful of military and civil engineers, surveyors, priests, merchants and other "amateurs" who designed churches, schools, commercial and public buildings during the 19th century. They brought with them the reigning styles of the West and adapted them to the local conditions in the manner of Coleman.

An early outstanding figure is John Turnbull Thomson, a surveyor, writer, artist and architect. Thomson arrived in Singapore in 1841 to take up the post of Government Surveyor for the Eastern Settlements. Not only did he make many surveys of, and plans for, the town, he supervised the laying of 24 miles of roads, including the one that bears his name. He also designed and built a number of structures for the government and private clients. Two which have survived to the present day are the Dalhousie Obelisk (1850) and the Horsburgh Lighthouse (1851). Thomson's sketches and paintings are an important record of the early days in the settlement. He left Singapore in 1853 for health reasons.

During the Thomson period a remarkable number of solid buildings began to replace the flimsy original ones, a sure sign of prosperity and permanence. These included many important temples and churches. The first St. Andrew's Cathedral was completed in 1836 (designed by Coleman); the first Roman Catholic Church on the site of the present St. Joseph's Institution in 1833 and the second, the Cathedral of the Good Shepherd, in 1846; Thian Hock Keng temple in Telok Ayer Street, circa 1842; and the Hajjah Fatimah Mosque in 1846. The Sri Mariamman Temple was rebuilt in brick to replace a wood and attap one, circa 1843, while the first Jewish synagogue was built in Synagogue Street in 1845.

Singapore in 1865

"The square itself (Commercial Square) is some 200 yards long by fifty broad, and many of the houses, or rather godowns (the latter term being used to denote mercantile establishments) which surround it, are of very elegant design. They are all built of brick and plastered over, but as both labour and materials have at no period since the settlement of the place been costly, their construction and finish is good. Some of the finest now standing are twenty or thirty years old. They are two stories high, lofty, and with heavy overleaning eaves; and the lower part of the front wall is composed of a series of arches or pillars inside of which a verandah runs from building to building. It appears that, in most cases, the early grants for town lands were in the nature of 99 and 999 years' leases, and imposed an obligation on the lessee to erect buildings with verandahs of a certain width for foot passengers. The clause seems, however, not to have been strictly adhered upon, and many of the verandahs were blocked up until about a year ago, when the municipal commissioners raised a point in the Supreme Court and obtained judgement in their favour. Since then, the verandahs have been kept tolerably clear . . . The town extends in very few points more than a mile from the beach, and, being remarkably compact, the country may be said to come right up to its walls. There are none of those intermediate, half-formed streets, with straggling houses here and there, separated by blank, barren, open spaces, which so often disfigure the outskirts of a town. Where the town ends, the country commences; indeed it would be difficult for a piece of ground to remain long desert, for nature would soon crowd it with her works, if man did not with his."

–John Cameron, Our Tropical Possessions in Malayan India (1865).

Convict Labour

"We found that the skill of the convicts never failed them and their capacity as builders and carpenters never seemed to slacken."

J.F.A. McNair, Prisoners Their Own Wardens (1899).

Already by the 1830s' Singapore had gained a reputation as "The Queen of the Further East" with the fine godowns and houses for her prosperous merchants some of her regal qualities. But despite these wonders and the city's orderly planning; vibrant commerce and lovely setting, many parts of the city were downright unsightly and unpleasant. Floods were frequent in the swampy lowlands and fires were a constant menace. Polluted water and open drains caused several cholera and smallpox epidemics, while stray dogs and dead ponies were left to rot on the beach. The roads were littered with garbage and the city's refuse thrown into swamps. Feeble coconut-oil lamps provided light after dark – gas lamps were introduced in the 1860s and electric lamps circa 1906. Pollution and stench were major blights.

The problem was money, writes C.M. Turnbull, in *A History of Singapore 1819-1975*: "Residents demanded more amenities but refused to pay higher property assessment, while the Calcutta-based East India Company government did not consider that the lightly-taxed Singapore deserved further government subsidies. They refused to build a new bridge near the mouth or to mend the two existing bridges which could not cope with traffic and were in a dangerous state of repair."

Another characteristic of the 19th century was the chronic labour shortage. A major portion of the construction force came from imported Indian convict labour. In 1825 the first lot of about 200 convicts were transferred from Bencoolen. Later they came directly from India. Under the hot sun the men (and some women) cleared land, cut trees, built roads, made bricks and other building materials, turned swamps into solid ground, reclaimed land and worked at construction sites. At any one time there were about one thousand convicts in Singapore. They were generally under the authority of a succession of engineer-architect army officers, mainly from the Madras Artillery, each of whom doubled up as the Superintendent of Public Works and Overseer of Convicts.

One interesting figure was Major J.F.A. McNair who designed what is now the Istana building and supervised the rebuilding of St. Andrew's Cathedral. McNair arrived in Singapore in 1856. In 1857 he was appointed Executive Engineer and Superintendent of Convicts, a post he held until 1873 when the jail was abolished. Upon his retirement McNair wrote about the Singapore penal system in a book entitled *Prisoners Their Own Wardens*.

Although the policy of using Singapore as a penal colony was revised in 1860, the convict labourers were present until 1873. Under McNair's supervision and the Public Works Department, the government embarked on an ambitious building programme in the 1860s. Projects included the Government Secretariat in 1865, now the Immigration Department; the remodelling of St. Andrew's Cathedral in 1858-61; and the Istana in 1869. Government House, as it was called then, was modelled on the basic form of a Malay house but enlarged to super-scale and adorned with Classical elements. It is an excellent example of the adaptation of the Palladian theme to suit the tropics.

On the building of St. Andrew's Cathedral

"The interior walls and columns were coated with a composition which has kept its colour and has set so very hard that it is almost impossible to drive a nail into it . . . It is Madras chunam made from shell lime without sand, but with this lime we had whites of eggs and coarse sugar, or "jaggery" beaten together to form a sort of paste, and mixed with water in which the husks of coconuts had been steeped. The walls were plastered with this composition, and after a certain period for drying, were rubbed with rock crystal or rounded stone until they took a beautiful polish, being occasionally dusted with fine soapstone powder and so leaving a remarkably smooth and glossy surface."

– Referring to the years 1862-63, on the building of St. Andrew's Cathedral as quoted in An Anecdotal History of Old Times in Singapore, 1819-1865.

The last three decades of the 19th century witnessed Singapore's transformation from an isolated settlement, with a somewhat precarious future, to a secure, important and bustling entrepôt port. Two significant events brought about what was to be the first of three building booms and ensured that the city's infrastructure expanded hand in hand with burgeoning commerce.

The first factor was the opening of the Suez Canal in 1869. East-west trade boomed as the travelling time between Europe and the East shortened. Trade expanded eight-fold in the period from 1873 to 1913. By 1903 Singapore was the world's seventh largest port in terms of tonnage of shipping. Secondly, in 1867, rule was transferred from India to the Colonial Office in London. The move brought many long-term benefits, including a better managed city.

The unprecedented prosperity brought with it a proliferation of activity that altered the physical appearance of the city. Dreams of wealth attracted an ever-increasing number of immigrants from China, India and Europe in search of fortune. By 1871 the population had risen to 97,000 and by 1900 to 228,000. The expanding population placed greater demands upon the town itself. Up to the 1870s-1880s the urban area had remained much as it was four decades earlier. But by the turn of the century it was bursting out of its confines, stretching through fields, jungle and plantations via new roads to Tanglin, Serangoon, Katong, Pasir Panjang and beyond. Wealthy Europeans and Chinese built their spacious, comfortable villas away from the crowded city while the poor and indentured labourers crowded in town tenements. Wealthy Chinese businessmen provided some amenities in the form of philanthropy. One was Cheang Hong Lim who gave $3,000 in 1876 to build a much-needed green in Chinatown which bears his name.

In town, land was reclaimed in Telok Ayer Bay between 1879 to 1887. Cavenagh Bridge opened in 1869 to link Commercial Square and the government quarters on the opposite bank of the river's mouth. Marshes in Tanjong Pagar and beyond were drained and the former nutmeg plantation, which lay between the new harbour (constructed in 1852) and the town, gave way to building along Tanjong Pagar and Neil Road. Along Boat Quay, Collyer Quay and Commercial Square, the older two-storey commercial buildings began to be replaced by bigger and taller structures – although businessmen still observed the comings and goings of ships through telescopes until the early 20th century when the introduction of the telephone rendered this practice obsolete and enabled business offices to move away from the sea front.

The government continued its building programme to accommodate the expanding administration of the town. In 1882, the General Hospital and Central Police Station were built, and in 1886 the National Museum and Coleman Bridge. The Assembly House, today's Parliament building, was extended in 1875 and the Esplanade was widened by reclaiming land from the sea to form the present Connaught Drive. The steam tramway was introduced in 1886 to ease the congestion of the motley assortment of vehicles on the roads. It was replaced by the Singapore Electric Tramway Company in 1905.

Skilled Craftsmanship

"Skilled craftsmanship played an important part in the excellent quality of the finished product and these early buildings reflect the opulence of the owners . . . further, and of great significance, they illustrate the high competence of Chinese craftsmanship that was brought into the building industry in Singapore from the late 19th century onwards, especially in the fields of carpentry, joinery, carving and decorative plasterwork. A corps of efficient craftsmen and foremen developed (using particularly Chinese tools and methods, incidentally) that formed the core of the support force that translated the architects' concepts into actual buildings in Singapore."

– Seow Eu Jin, The Architectural Development of Singapore.

Then in 1887, the Municipal Ordinance was passed. The town area was separated from the rural districts and put under the direct control of the government. The Ordinance also led to the systematic naming of roads. Signboards were placed at the corner of every street. The signboards were inscribed with "the name by which the street shall be known". Confusion arose. Most of the names given by the municipality to the various streets were used only by the European portion of the population and were ignored by the rest. Around the same time, formal submission of building plans for approval by the Municipal Government also became compulsory. It was a timely move. Buildings were becoming bigger and taller and several incidents of structural collapse were reported.

Up until the 1880s most buildings were the work of amateurs, quasi-professionals or skilled craftsmen. The first listing of "architect" in *The Straits Times Almanack, Calendar and Directory* was in 1860, one William Edwards of Prinsep Street. In 1884 the firm of Lermit and Annamalai, Architects and Surveyors, was listed. Mr A.W. Lermit, a surveyor from London, left his Singapore Tamil Surveyor partner in 1888 and joined Mr A.A. Swan. When Mr Lermit parted company with Mr Swan, Mr J.W.B. Maclaren was made a partner and the firm changed its name to Swan and Maclaren, as it is still known today. Swan and Maclaren is Singapore's oldest firm of architects.

It was in 1895 that the man destined to be the firm's leading figure for the next 15 years – and perhaps the most potent force in Singapore since Coleman – joined the firm: Regent Alfred John Bidwell. Bidwell had been placed on the honours list for design at his school in London and had worked with a London firm before coming out to Malaya to join the Public Works Department in Selangor. While he was there, he worked on the Saracenic Government Secretariat. Selangor's loss proved to be Singapore's gain. Under Bidwell's supervision the firm developed a rich, robust style which has been called by Professor Seow Eu Jin, former Head of the National University of Singapore School of Architecture, as "Neo-Renaissance".

In 1899 the firm completed the main wing of the Raffles Hotel. The project established their reputation as undisputed leaders in design. Other major commissions followed and some of Mr Bidwell's buildings still remain. These include the Teutonia Club, built in 1900, now part of the Goodwood Hotel; Stamford House, Victoria Memorial Hall and Chased El Synagogue all constructed in 1905; the Singapore Cricket Club extensions in 1906 and St. Joseph's Church in 1913.

In 1902 Mr Tian Tye Ho, the owner of two shophouses in Pagoda Street, decided to turn his two-storey structures into three-storeys and enhance their facades. He asked the firm of Tomlinson and Tian Fook to draw up and submit plans. Mr Tian was just one of over a thousand people who submitted a record number of building plans to the municipal authorities that year, the kick-off of Singapore's second major building boom. (The third came in the early 1970s). Today Mr Tian's plans can be seen among the collection of early building plans housed in the National Archives.

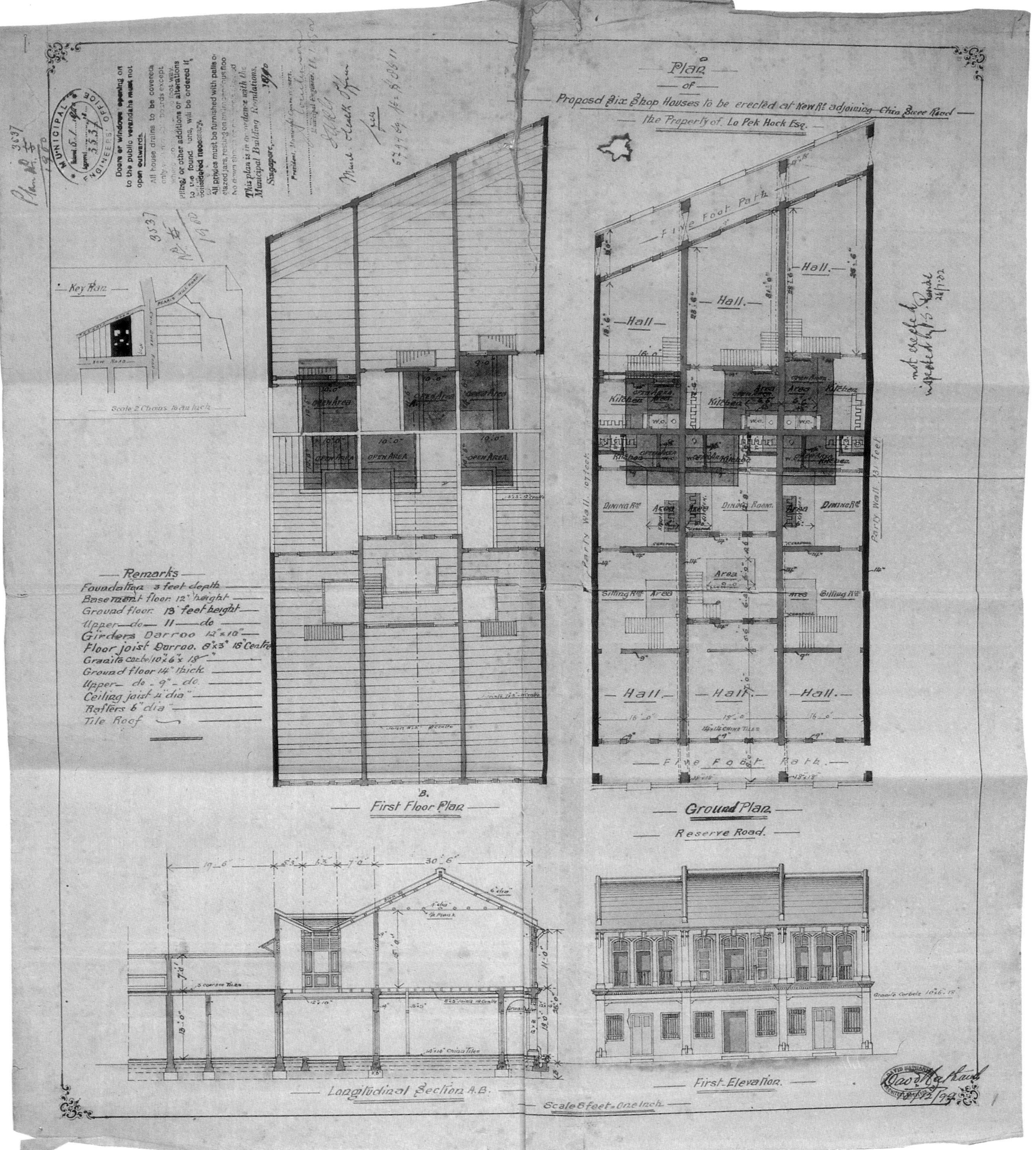

LEFT: *A turn of the century building plan from the National Archives.*

The 1900s

"The town is well laid out, and the streets are broad and well cared for. The interior of the island is undulating and consists of numerous hills of from 50 to 80 feet high, with narrow valleys between, and on these the European and Chinese residents have built houses, surrounding them with gardens of fruit trees and flowers."

– *W.H.M. Read, Play and Politics (1901).*

Many of the historic old buildings which remain today were built during this period, including many fine examples of the shophouse or its residential counterpart, the terrace house, both of which are scattered throughout Singapore's long-established urban areas.

There is, in fact, no type of building more associated with Singapore than these unique terraces and shophouses, with their ornate facades of Chinese, Malay and European Classical details. Built in a style called Straits Chinese, Palladian Chinese or Chinese Baroque architecture, they are as eclectic and cosmopolitan as the city itself. They grew, like Singapore, from humble, hardworking origins: the very utilitarian Chinese shophouse with living and working quarters together, brought to Singapore from Southern China via Malacca by the Straits-born Chinese. There are still many fine examples in Malacca on Jalan Tan Cheng Lock and Jalan Tranquerah.

The earliest shophouses in Singapore were simple, unadorned timber buildings with attap roofs and the sites allotted to the population for building them tended to be narrow. The more ornate and elaborate residential terrace houses made their appearance with the rise of the wealthy Chinese merchant families from the late 19th century onwards, especially among the Straits-born, or Peranakan Community. The entire material culture of the "Nonyas" and "Babas" evolved into an eclectic hybrid of Chinese, Malay and European Classical elements, from food and dress, to interior decor and furniture, and so it was with their architecture.

TOP AND ABOVE: Two elevational drawings showing intricate window designs.

It is fair to say that until World War II, the terrace house dominated domestic architecture. The more or less standard floor plan was given variation in the treatment of the details. Until the 1880s the houses would have been built by Chinese or Indian contractors who would have relied on standard plans in pattern books, as was the practice in many parts of the world then. Around the turn of the century and later, European architects and engineers designed the buildings for the Straits Chinese, freely plagiarising Western architectural motifs. There is a good stock of streets with excellent "intact" terrace houses of excellent quality in Blair Road, Emerald Hill, Geylang and Joo Chiat, Syed Alwi and Petain Roads, Jalan Besar and in the streets emanating from Serangoon Road, as the reader will see on the pages that follow.

But fashions change, technology improves, economic considerations rise and there are more demands on the city to cope with an expanding population, the different modes of transport and the changing socio-political climate.

By the 1920s many parts of "suburbia" had been firmly established. While Kampong Glam retained its Arab-Malay ambiance, Malay settlements had expanded up and down the coastline, eastward to Katong, Siglap, Bedok, Geylang Serai and Changi; and westward to Telok Blangah, Pasir Panjang and Jurong. The Indian community, first prominent in Chulia and Market Streets, was entrenched in High Street, Serangoon Road and the railway and port areas of Tanjong Pagar and Keppel Road as well as around the naval base in Sembawang. The Chinese had

Chinese Dwelling House, postcard circa 1900.

Singapore. Chinese Dwelling House

dispersed inland while the Europeans had moved from their central enclaves of Beach Road and Fort Canning to Tanglin and Holland Roads. The British authorities also set up military complexes at Changi, Alexandra, Ayer Rajah and at Seletar. The number of motorcars increased from 842 in 1915 to 3,506 in 1920, causing acute congestion on the roads.

The early years of the 20th century also saw the introduction of important technological innovations which changed forever the architectural equation, including electricity, modern sanitation, reinforced concrete, lifts, rudimentary airconditioning and structural steel.

By 1923 the architectural profession itself was becoming more organised. By 1927 all buildings had to be designed by qualified architects, who were remunerated a certain percentage as fee. When the Architects Ordinance was passed 46 professionals registered on the rolls immediately.

By the 1930s a new breed of architects, with a different approach learnt in England and Europe, arrived. They began to depart from the Classical tradition and experimented with the new technology and the aesthetics of Modern architecture. The first glimmer of the new wave is seen in buildings like Kallang Airport Terminal, Clifford Pier, Shaw's Building, Fullerton Building and the Railway Station, as well as in the Chinese-Spanish houses designed by the talented Frank Brewer, the man who also designed the Cathay Building, Singapore's first skyscraper.

One interesting development during this period was the formation of the Singapore Improvement Trust in 1927, a government statutory body and the forerunner of the Housing and Development Board which was formed in 1960. The SIT carried out some slum clearance in the 1930s but the momentum was disrupted when Japanese bombs fell on the city.

The advent of modern architecture coincided with the onset of The Great Depression. One very concrete result of the changed circumstances was an acute awareness of economics as the prime determinant of design. Although terrace houses continued to be built, new building dictates – and economics – produced a simpler style.

All of these factors – the Depression, the advances in technology, new influences in design and aesthetics as well as new demands on the city itself – sounded the death knell of Singapore's traditional eclectic architecture. World War II and subsequent severe housing problems ensured that it would never be rekindled.

In recent years the city has changed at an exciting pace. Nineteen pre-war buildings have been gazetted as "monuments" by the Preservation of Monuments Board since 1970. Yet more old buildings are well-loved, well-kept landmarks. But many architectural treasures have disappeared in the wake of rapid urban renewal and the future of what remains of Singapore's architectural heritage has yet to be decided.

PENINSULA
VICTORIA THEATRE

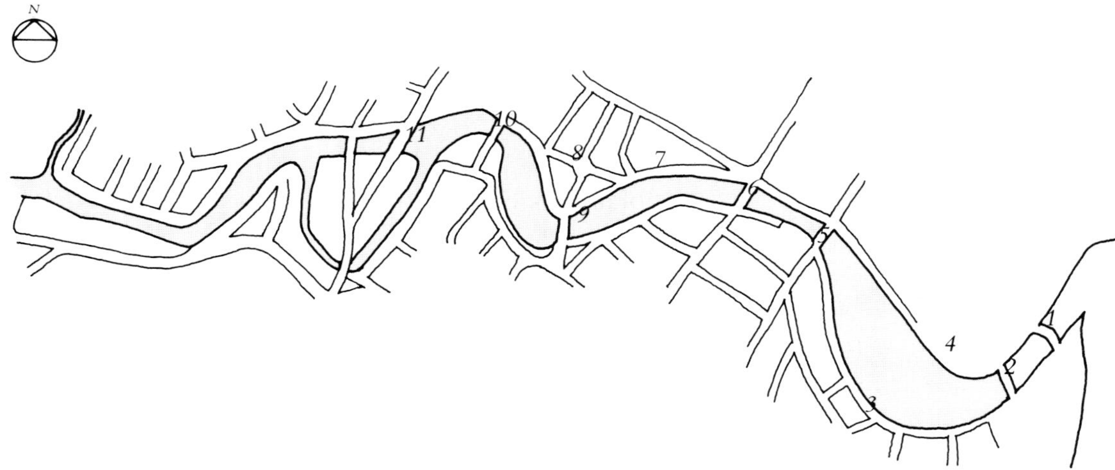

1 Anderson Bridge
2 Cavenagh Bridge
3 South Boat Quay
4 Empress Place
5 Elgin Bridge
6 Coleman Bridge
7 North Boat Quay
8 Circus at junction of Read Street and Clarke Street
9 Read Bridge
10 Ord Bridge
11 Clemenceau Bridge

BOAT QUAY

The silhouette of the Singapore River buildings, and especially the crescent of South Boat Quay, have been a familiar sight to generations of Singaporeans. Despite pockets of redevelopment, clustered mostly around the mouth of the river, the area still retains a remarkable continuity with the past and a charm all of its own.

When Raffles landed in 1819, the river bank was lined with dense mangrove swamps. Only today's Empress Place was terra firma. The Orang Laut (pirates) lived in floating settlements upriver, while the Malays lived in wooden huts dominated by the Temenggong's house at the mouth of the river.

Raffles was determined to see the 2 km-long river become the heart of the settlement. In his 1822-23 Town Plan he designated the north bank for use by the government — and so it is today. The south bank near the river mouth was set aside for the use of merchants. In 1823 Commercial Square (renamed Raffles Place in 1858) was carved out of a hillock. The earth from the hillock was used to fill in the swampy south bank and create South Boat Quay. The early merchants located their warehouses and offices along this stretch of the river and built their own private jetties for easier loading and unloading.

Singapore's free port status set the pace for the river's rapid development from the river mouth upstream to Robertson Quay. By the 1840s the river was too congested and the merchants complained. Some even said Raffles had made a mistake in siting the town there since space for commerce was cramped. A new harbour was built at Tanjong Pagar in 1852 and, although several firms were quick to make use of it, three quarters of all shipping business in the 1860s was still done at Boat Quay.

It was the widespread use of the steamer ship (first used in 1827) after the 1869 opening of the Suez Canal which most affected life on the river. Traffic dwindled for a few years but, as shipping demands at the new harbour began to exceed wharf

"From the river's entrance to this bridge (Lord Elgin Bridge) on the town side, a long range of godowns extend, forming a complete crescent. Those nearer the entrance are occupied by Europeans, but all the godowns further up are the property of Chinese; and though the whole range is pretty much of a character as far as the buildings are concerned, yet the Chinese division is the more imposing on account of the bright colours which adorn the walls . . . At night the view of these houses is still more interesting, all the verandahs and windows being lit up with many coloured Chinese lanterns, the effect of which is doubled by the reflection of the placid water that flows past their doors.
On the eastern bank of the river for a considerable way up there are no houses, the land having been reserved for Government purposes . . . The crescent of buildings which I have described, and which is about a quarter of a mile long, is termed Boat Quay from the fact of nearly the entire river frontage opposite them being taken up with the loading and discharging of cargo boats."

– John Cameron, Our Tropical Possessions in Malayan India (1865).

space, it recovered and the system was started of using lighters, or tongkangs, towed by powered tugs in and out of the river to vessels at sea.

The mouth of the river saw the most change, with not infrequent demolition, rebuilding and land reclamation. Around the bridges the odd godown was removed for widening of roads or replacing of bridge spans. But from the late 1800s to the middle of the 20th century the river silhouette stayed basically the same.

Two types of buildings dominate either side of the Boat Quay landscape: shophouses and warehouses, or godowns. The shophouses dominate the mid-river front along both North and South Boat Quay. Most of the narrow, deep, shophouses are two-storey but several have third-storey verandahs. They were built over a period of time and some are elaborate while others are exceedingly simple.

The first godowns were built in the 1820s and, until the advent of modern architecture, their design remained fairly constant. They had to be big, well-ventilated, dry, clean and built for easy access to the tongkangs. Their simply designed facades conceal vast uncluttered spaces of storage space. The early godowns represented a marriage of east and west: double storied Doric columns, rounded arches, tall windows, entablatures and Chinese roof tiles in Palladian symmetry adapted to the tropical merchant milieu. There is an excellent example of an early Chinese godown at No. 13 Clarke Quay.

Linda Berry, in her book *Singapore's River, A Living Legacy*, has pointed out that the death knell for the river as a working waterway was sounded long ago. For more than a century it had faced difficulties — like pollution and congestion and the fact that parts of the river were too shallow for moorage at low tide — which eventually spelled its doom. She cites as parallel examples the problems faced by the grand old markets of London's Convent Garden and Les Halles in Paris. These colourful, historic centres of a similar life of trade and bartering were forced to move to upgrade their facilities and allow for better development and use of the downtown core areas.

In the same way, progress has nudged the lighters and bumboats to other localities, but some of the historical buildings nestled along the river's edge still remain.

The Singapore River, circa 1843-47. This view from the mouth of the river looks towards Fort Canning and shows the first Government House. The building on the right is a landing shed, originally designed as a coach house.

IAN C. STEWART

LEFT: Cavenagh Bridge was built in 1869 to provide a link for vehicles between the Government offices and Commercial Square (Raffles Place). The elegant steel frame of the suspension bridge was manufactured by P. & W. Maclellan, Engineers, of Glasgow, Scotland who also built the Telok Ayer Market. The bridge, the last major project undertaken by Indian convict labourers here, is named after Colonel Sir Orfeur Cavenagh, the last Governor of Singapore appointed by the East India Company. Today Cavenagh Bridge is one of nine bridges built between 1869 and 1920 spanning the river. It only serves pedestrian traffic.

BELOW: The crescent of Boat Quay has been a familiar sight to generations of Singaporeans.

IAN C. STEWART

R. IAN LLOYD

R. IAN LLOYD

FAR LEFT: Window details of No. 53 South Boat Quay.

LEFT AND BELOW: Boat Quay area facade details were inspired by aesthetics and superstitions both East and West.

IAN C. STEWART

IAN C. STEWART

IAN C. STEWART

ABOVE: Nos. 56, 57, 58, 60 and 61 South Boat Quay. Many of the shophouses along the river front have third-storey verandahs, reminiscent of European riverside residences with a viewing gallery.

IAN C STEWART

LEFT: *The Ellenborough building (1845) designed by J.T. Thomson. The facades of the block of shophouses, built as a unified group between Ellenborough Street, Fish Street and Boat Quay, have been largely obliterated through successive alterations. But the original Classical details can still be discerned in the arched doorway and columns shown here. When new, the building was considered something special. Said a newspaper report of the time: ". . . and Tan Tock Seng is far advanced with the erection of an extensive range of shops on a uniform plan and with pretentions to architectural beauty than the general run of such boutiques. This quarter is to bear the name of Ellenborough Buildings!"*

BELOW: *More three-storey buildings along South Boat Quay. While not architecturally outstanding, they illustrate the appealing scale of vernacular architecture in relation to the river and the steps of the quay.*

R. IAN LLOYD

The roofs of North Boat Quay. The streets of this warehouse area have many of the qualities of a small village streetscape. Note the Chinese roofline of the warehouse, No. 13 Read Street.

R. IAN LLOYD

IAN C. STEWART

Three views of the Tan Si Chong Su, No. 15 Magazine Road. The small, ornate temple was built by Hokkien merchant philanthropists Tan Kim Cheng, eldest son of Singapore pioneer Tan Tock Seng, and Tan Beng Swee, the son of another well-known 19th century businessman, Tan Kim Seng. The exterior of the temple (far left) shows two characteristic features of Southern Chinese architecture: the exaggerated roof curve and the elaborately carved brackets which support the roof. The main courtyard (left) of the compound has carved granite pillars framing the altar.

The historic warehouses of Boat Quay were built to serve one of commerce's most humble needs: storing goods. Yet these buildings were often elevated to a nobility far beyond their scale and function. This was achieved through the use of simple Classical forms, such as the arched verandahways shown here.

R. IAN LLOYD

R. IAN LLOYD

R. IAN LLOYD

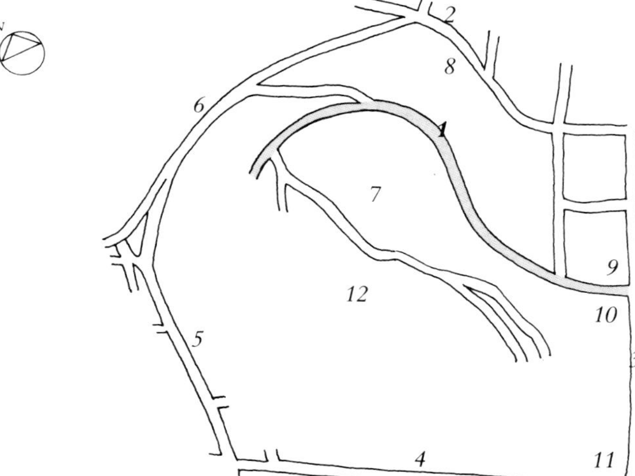

1 *Canning Rise*
2 *Stamford Road*
3 *Hill Street*
4 *River Valley Road*
5 *Clemenceau Avenue*
6 *Fort Canning Road*
7 *Old Christian Cemetery*
8 *National Museum*
9 *Armenian Church*
10 *Central Fire Station*
11 *National Archives*
12 *Fort Canning Reservoir*

FORT CANNING

Legend has it that in ancient Singapura the hill we now call Fort Canning was a splendid forest shielding palaces and royal courts. When Raffles landed, the fort was in ruins and the local population believed it to be haunted by ghosts. They called it Bukit Larangan, the Forbidden Hill and, indeed, the keramat, or tomb, of the last ruler of ancient Singapura, Sultan Iskander Shah, is there.

Over the years the function of the hill has changed but it has been a vital central feature of modern urban Singapore from the start. First, it was called Government Hill. Undaunted by superstition, Raffles had the first government house built there in 1823 and he lived in it during the 10 months of his last visit. The flimsy wood and attap bungalow was later extended and became the home of the senior British official, the Resident Councillor. Raffles also started the first Botanic Gardens in 1822 on the hill, looked after by the famed botanist from Calcutta, Nathaniel Wallich. The gardens were closed in 1829 due to a shortage of funds.

The hill was also the site of the first Christian cemetery. At first the cemetery was located in front of the Resident's House, an uncomfortable arrangement no doubt, so new grounds were consecrated further down the hill in 1834. The cemetery was moved to Bukit Timah and the Resident's House demolished when the military took possession of the hill in 1857. They renamed it Fort Canning, after the Governor General of India, and built a 2.86 ha fort as part of the efforts to boost defence. Completed in 1860, the fort was considered a folly from the beginning and it was demolished in 1907 to make way for the present reservoir. Only the gates of the old fort remain.

Today the hill is a serene park. Old British barracks have been turned into squash courts and a restaurant. Some of the old tombstones have been brought back, to be joined by modern sculptures by ASEAN artists. And around the foot of the hill are nestled many low-rise buildings housing important activities, including the National Library and Museum; the Van Kleef Aquarium; the Hill Street Police and Fire stations; the Registry of Marriages; the Drama Centre and the Wesley Methodist Church.

IAN C. STEWART

ABOVE: *One of two Gothic Revival gateways, which originally led to a Christian cemetery, designed by Captain Charles Faber (of Mount Faber fame) shortly after his arrival here in 1844. An engineer by training who took up the post of Government Engineer, Faber, in all likelihood, copied the design from architectural pattern books published in Britain by the leading proponents of the day. The completion of the gateways in 1846 marked the introduction of the Gothic Revival style into Singapore, a theme later expressed more fully in many other buildings, including St Andrew's Cathedral and the chapel of the Convent of the Holy Infant Jesus.*

RIGHT: *Two monuments in Classical design over unknown graves may have been designed by G.D. Coleman.*

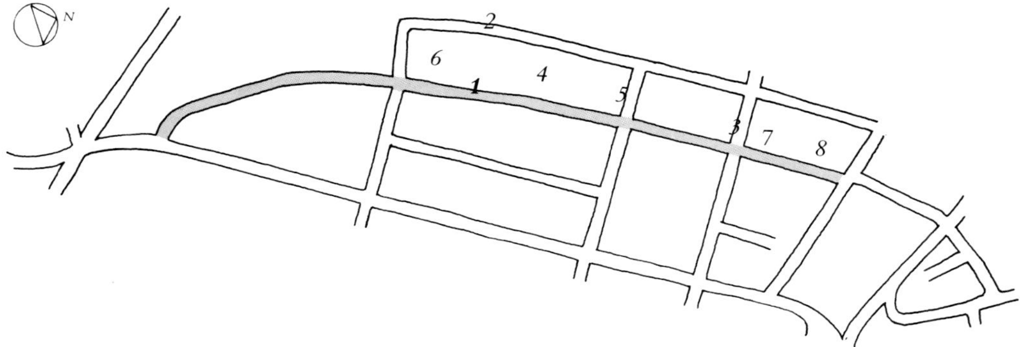

1 *Telok Ayer Street*
2 *Amoy Street*
3 *Cross Street*
4 *Thian Hock Keng*
5 *Nagoor Durga Shrine*
6 *Al-Abrar Mosque*
7 *Ying He Hui Guan*
8 *Fuk Tak Ch'i*

TELOK AYER STREET

Telok Ayer Street once ran close to and parallel with the original seashore and formed the base of the Chinese settlement dictated by Raffles. It was not only one of the first streets of the town but was also one of the most important in Chinatown and, indeed, in all of Singapore from the 1820s until the 1880s.

One indication of this is the number of religious buildings and Clan associations erected during the early years, including the Thian Hock Keng Temple in 1839-42; the South Indian Muslim-built Nagore Durgha Shrine in 1828-30; the Al Abrar Mosque established in 1827 (although the brick building was not erected until 1850-55) and the Ying He Hui Guan, the Hakka Association Hall, in 1843.

The other main building form along the street is the ubiquitious shophouse. When land was originally portioned out in Singapore it was mainly as plots for residential compound houses. But in some of the central areas these plots were carved up into long, narrow strips with as little as 4.8m frontage and as deep as 45.7m. The width was originally determined by the available length of timber felled. The design yielded the maximum area possible from the narrow frontage.

The early shophouses were "imported" from China either directly or by the Straits Chinese families who came down to Singapore from Malacca. From the beginning, many Chinese family businesses in Singapore had close personal ties with Malacca. As more China-born immigrants arrived, the character of Telok Ayer Street changed. Between 1850 and 1870, it was notorious as a centre for the Chinese slave trade. Between 1879 and 1887, Telok Ayer Bay was filled in with earth from the nearby hillocks, including Mount Wallich, creating the land which forms the Robinson Road, Anson Road area. By the 1890s, Telok Ayer had become noisy and congested, sending the wealthier and more established families in search of better accommodation further out of town.

Today Telok Ayer is still predominantly lined by two and three storey shophouses, including some built during the time when skilled craftsmanship in building and construction was at its best.

"The whole of the native part of the town . . . and the river frontage I have described, are very much alike in appearances. The buildings are closely packed together and of a uniform height and character. The style is a sort of compromise between English and Chinese. The walls are of brick, plastered over, and the roofs are covered with tiles. The windows are of lattice woodwork – there being no glazing in this part of the world. Under the windows of many houses occupied by Chinese are very chaste designs of flowers or birds in porcelain. The ridges of roofs, too, and the eaves, are frequently similarly ornamented, and it is no unusual thing to see a perfect little garden of flowers and vegetables in boxes and pots exposed on the tops of the houses. Underneath run, for the entire length of the streets, the enclosed verandahs of which I spoke before, and in a quiet observant walk through these a very great deal may be learned . . ."

– John Cameron, Our Tropical Possessions in Malayan India (1865).

RIGHT: The 1856 painting by Percy Carpenter entitled "Singapore at Sunrise from Mount Wallich" shows a well-developed Telok Ayer Street lined with compact shophouses. Mount Wallich has long gone, the earth used to fill in Telok Ayer Bay. But Ann Siang Hill, directly behind the Telok Ayer area, is still a feature of the urbanscape.

RIGHT: Telok Ayer Street today. It is not so much the high quality of the architecture which gives the street a pleasant feeling but an historic quality which can still be felt.

FAR RIGHT: Original window details from No. 22 Amoy Street. The Chinese geometric pattern of the window panes can be seen in old houses in Malacca and Singapore. The same geometric pattern can also be seen on the glass paned doors of some antique cabinets.

R. IAN LLOYD

R. IAN LLOYD

R. IAN LLOYD

R. IAN LLOYD

LEFT: *Granite column bases from shophouse on Telok Ayer Street. On some of the earlier shophouses the bases of the first storey columns are carved out of solid granite imported from China.*

R. IAN LLOYD

IAN C. STEWART

LEFT: *The Ying He Hui Guan. This 19th century Hakka clan association building is one of the few non-temple buildings in pure Chinese style which remain in Singapore.*

ABOVE: *The building has an internal courtyard which allows for ventilation and natural daylight.*

1 New Bridge Road
2 Eu Tong Sen Street
3 Cross Street
4 Mosque Street
5 Pagoda Street
6 Temple Street
7 Smith Street
8 Sago Street
9 Trengganu Street
10 South Bridge Road
11 Sri Mariamman Temple
12 Jamae Mosque

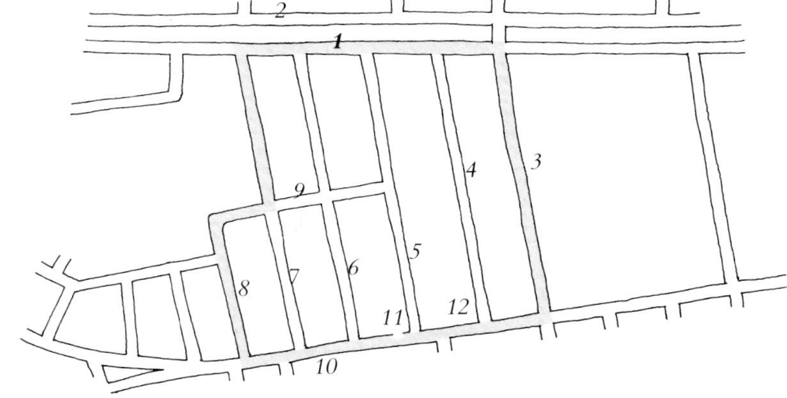

CHINATOWN

"As far as prosperity is concerned, no area in Singapore can compare with 'Greater Town'. All foreign firms, banks, Post Office and customs office are found along the seaside there. Although there are also bazaars in 'Lesser Town', they are set up by the natives to sell local products and various foodstuff. Not a single big market is found there . . . There is a place known as Kreta Ayer in Greater Town where restaurants, theatres and brothels are concentrated. It is the most populated area where filth and dirt are hidden. No place in Singapore can compare with it. Along the streets gas lamps are on throughout the night. In front of every shop, there is a divine lamp hung over the door."

– A Description of Singapore in 1887 by Li Chung-Chu, a Manchu official, as quoted in Chinatown "An Album of a Singapore Community" Archives and Oral History Department (1983).

Any book on Singapore's architectural heritage would be incomplete without the inclusion of Chinatown. The area is both historically important and architecturally rich, although many of the buildings are relatively dilapidated.

When Raffles landed in Singapore, there was already a small Chinese community established here. Their numbers swelled quickly. Anticipating that they would eventually form the largest segment of the population, he allotted the entire area south of the Singapore River beyond Commercial Square for their kampong when he introduced the Town Plan. By 1871 there were over 50,000 Chinese on the island.

By 1836 Chinatown stretched from the Singapore River west to Cross Street and from Telok Ayer Bay north to South Bridge Road. In 1840 much of the land around Pagoda Street was still in the hands of the East India Company. New Bridge Road was laid out about 1840-41 and in 1843 the Government started to issue land titles in the area. By 1857 Pagoda, Mosque, Smith, Temple – or Almeida as it was then known – and Sago Streets and Sago Lane were laid out. Some of this land was originally in the hands of the wealthy Portuguese d'Almeida family who began to sublease the originally freehold lands as smaller lots after 1859.

The years betwen 1860 and 1880 marked a period of rapid development for Chinatown. By 1890 the area was already densely populated. The influx was predominantly male. In 1836, for every 1,000 Chinese females, there were 14,642 males. By 1891 the ratio had improved somewhat and there were 4,680 Chinese males to 1,000 females. This perpetual imbalance had a tremendous impact on the lifestyle of the male migrants and the predominant housing was bachelor quarters. Many buildings were used as coolie lodging houses. In 1901, for example, out of 59 houses along Pagoda Street, 12 were used for this purpose.

Most of the houses standing today along these streets were built during the years from 1900 to 1941. Despite their humble and strenuous use, the buildings of Chinatown exhibit a sense of proportion and refinement of architectural details still considered exceptional by today's standards.

IAN C. STEWART

LEFT: The characteristic red roofs of Chinatown.

BELOW: The four-storey former Singapore Improvement Trust Government quarters for customs workers at Cross Street and New Bridge Road. Built in the early 1930s, the influence of modern architecture is apparent in the relatively plain facades. Yet the flavour of Chinatown's earlier shophouses is echoed in the retention of certain characteristic elements such as the sense of proportion and scale of the buildings, the narrow frontages of the individual units and the window treatment.

RIGHT: Mosque Street. Despite their presently shabby condition, the refined Classical details on the facades of these Mosque Street shophouses (part of a row of eight contiguous units) are still undeniably elegant.

R. IAN LLOYD

R. IAN LLOYD

Two views of Trengganu Street. Often thought of as the heart of Chinatown (it is the only full cross street in the area), it is given strong definition by the presence of the three storey shophouses built as a unified block between Smith and Temple Streets. A less Classical example of shophouse architecture, the building is made all the more unique by the presence of the overhanging third storey built entirely in timber.

LEFT: A 1910 photograph.
BELOW: A photograph taken in 1983 before the street stalls moved into new premises in the Kreta Ayer market complex.

BELOW: *Pagoda Street was already built-up by the 1860s but the present shophouses date from the early 20th century. Like many of Chinatown's buildings, they show the strains of decades of overcrowding and neglect. Yet their Classical details still make an elegant architectural statement. A strong sense of unity is created by the repetition of similar heights and facades along both sides of the street. The character of Pagoda Street and the quality of its architecture have fascinated Singaporeans and tourists alike. In 1972, Queen Elizabeth was brought for a stroll down this "museum" lane as part of her state visit.*

RIGHT: *Two architectural contributions made to Chinatown by millionaire businessman Eu Tong Sen. The "Art Deco" Majestic Theatre on Eu Tong Sen Street (right) was built in 1927. Designed by Swan and Maclaren it was used as a Cantonese opera theatre for many years. After World War II it was converted to a cinema and renamed first Queen's Theatre then Majestic Theatre. Below is a detail from the glazed ceramic tile panel which borders the front and side of the building. The Renaissance-inspired three storey shophouse along South Bridge Road (far right) is dated 1910 and houses a medicine business started by Mr Eu. It is symmetrical and has strong Classical elements. Even today the building is an imposing presence along the street.*

KOUO SHANG-WEI

IAN C. STEWART

IAN C. STEWART

R. IAN LLOYD

R. IAN LLOYD

LEFT: *One of Chinatown's most refined shophouses. The original plan for this three-storey structure with Venetian windows at the corner of South Bridge Road and Ramah Street calls it "Proposed photographer's house . . . the property of Lee Yin Fan Esq." and is dated 1900. The plan also gives a clue to the building technology of the day. The foundation was to be made from "Good lime concrete composed of 4 parts broken bricks, 2 parts good sand and 1 part good lime".*

R. IAN LLOYD

R. IAN LLOYD

ABOVE: *Two more of Chinatown's unexpected delights. Unusual timber fretwork frames the third storeys of Nos. 11 and 13 Smith Street (top). Nos. 44–46 Smith Street (bottom) have an open arched third-storey. Note the displacement of the columns between second and third storeys to allow the larger arched opening in the centre.*

1 Ann Siang Hill
2 Ann Siang Road
3 Club Street
4 Erskine Road
5 Kadayanallur Road
6 South Bridge Road

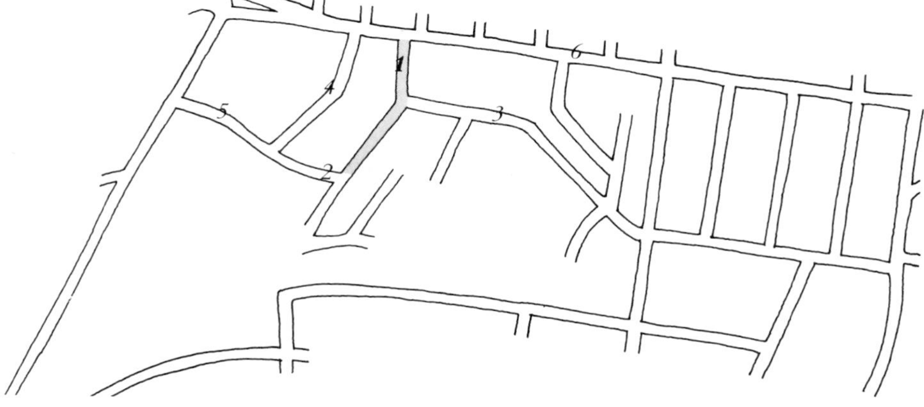

ANN SIANG HILL

Ann Siang Hill was first known as Scott's Hill after its owner Mr Charles Scott who cultivated nutmeg and cloves there. On his death, his wife sold the land to Mr Ann Siang, a rich sawmiller after whom the street is named. This high ground conveniently located behind the more densely populated Telok Ayer and Amoy Streets soon became a popular location for clan associations.

Today, Ann Siang Hill's charm stems from the assymetrical layout of the streets, so unlike most modern streetscapes, and the sloping gradient of the terrain. The buildings were constructed between 1903 and 1940 and many are in reasonably good condition. The oldest building is No. 81 Club Street designed by H.W. Chung and presently the premises of Kong Beng Book Co. The clubhouse at No. 84 Club Street was designed in 1919 by J.B. Westerhout, a prolific architect of the time, but has since been renovated.

Within the area one finds an interesting mixture of styles representative of those that prevailed over three decades, such as the various permutations and combinations of full and half length windows.

Although fashions changed, the main features of the shophouse remained consistent. Each unit has a narrow frontage, measuring between 4.8m and 6m, and a depth as extensive as 30.5m to 45.7m. In the older versions there is a series of courtyards, but these gradually degenerated into small airwells. All of the houses have pitched roofs with red clay tiles and all have a verandah or five foot way, a feature which may hark back to the original Town Plan and Raffles instructions that ". . . each house should have a verandah of a certain depth, open at all times as a continued covered passage on each side of the street."

Backlanes appeared only after 1907. In that year a Professor W.J. Simpson from England reported on the sanitary conditions of the town. The population then stood at less than a quarter of a million, but overcrowding was a common feature in the congested town area so the Municipal Ordinance was amended to make backlanes a mandatory requirement.

R. IAN LLOYD

No. 48 Club Street, an enchanting combination of East and West. The there panels of Chinese characters, originally in glass paillettes and now painted over, and a Chinese-style frieze between the first and second storey, also painted over, are combined with European elements such as the fan light windows on the third storey and centrally placed French doors.

BELOW: Club Street. The curved and inclined terrain of this street creates a distinctive pleasant environment.

BOTTOM: Nos. 12 to 26 Ann Siang Road. A series of three-storey building of the late 1920s in concrete built by different owners yet sharing a pleasing uniformity in the relative simplicity of their facades. No. 14 has a prominent cantilevered balcony.

BELOW: Exceptionally fine gilt pintu pagar at No. 33 Ann Siang Road. The painted plaster scrolls are in original condition and the two pairs of gilt-trimmed window shutters are enhanced with calligraphy couplets — a delightful composition.

R. IAN LLOYD

R. IAN LLOYD

R. IAN LLOYD

BELOW: *No. 37 Club Street, designed by Frank Brewer. Brewer was one of the early architects in Singapore in the 1920s and 1930s trained in the aesthetics of Modern architecture who broke away from Classical idioms. His trademark includes simple proportions, steeply pitched roofs and an interesting treatment of exterior plasterwork. Even though the building here includes Chinese elements it has, even today, a distinctly "modern" feel to it. Brewer designed many houses and commercial buildings including the Cathay Building, Singapore's first skyscraper.*

BELOW: *The corner position of this simple four-storey concrete 1924 building at No. 37 Erskine Road has been exploited to the fullest. The central "tower" enhances the symmetry of the building and gives added drama to the corner.*

R. IAN LLOYD

R. IAN LLOYD

R. IAN LLOYD

R. IAN LLOYD

LEFT ABOVE: *The doorways of Ann Siang Hill. No. 26 Ann Siang Road (far left) was built in 1926 and has a two panel pintu pagar framed by a heavily tiled facade. No. 13 Ann Siang Road (centre) dates from 1931 and shows the bar sliding door, a feature of many buildings in the area. No. 9 on the same road (near left) also has a folding two-panel pintu pagar.*

LEFT: *Nos. 12, 14, 16 and 18 Club Street, built in 1928. More pastel portraits.*

1 *Neil Road*
2 *Tanjong Pagar*
3 *Keong Saik Road*
4 *Bukit Pasoh*
5 *New Bridge Road*
6 *Duxton Plain Parkway*
7 *Jinrikisha Building*
8 *Yan Kit Swimming Complex*

NEIL ROAD

R. IAN LLOYD

One of the many faces of the Neil Road area. This blue and white elevation is from Keong Saik Street.

The streets immediately to the west of, and bordering on, Chinatown are still reasonably intact and contain many fine examples of the Singapore Eclectic style of architecture. The irregular skyline and the wide variety of styles illustrate clearly the fact that the city is the product of generations rather than individuals – from the turn-of-the-century three-storey buildings along the Tanjong Pagar with their more Classical features to those at No. 11 to 23 Bukit Pasoh, built of reinforced concrete with cantilevered balconies between 1933 and 1937.

The area developed much later than Chinatown. Seven ha of it was a flourishing nutmeg plantation advertised for sale in 1856 in the newspaper. The plantation was centred on Duxton Hill, one of several hillocks which slowed the expansion of the town westward. Neil Road, the first track laid in the vicinity, was known in Chinese as "the steep street of Kreta Ayer" and it led to the Temenggong's village at Telok Blangah.

Development along Tanjong Pagar was closely linked to the growth of steamship activities at Tanjong Pagar docks from 1861 onwards. The road became one of the main thoroughfares for goods moving between riverside warehouses and the new docks. Bukit Pasoh was formerly known as Bukit Padre and over the years many trade associations selected sites along the road for their headquarters.Duxton Plain Parkway, which runs parallel to Bukit Pasoh crossing under Neil Road, was once a railway reserve and remains a pleasant urban green space.

The majority of the houses along the streets in this area were built between 1890 and 1940. Until the 1880s, when it became necessary to submit building plans to the Municipal Authority, most of the terrace houses would have been built probably by Chinese contactors using standard building plans or pattern books, and the Chinese elements were more pronounced.

From the 1890s to the 1920s, the designs are mainly attributable to British-educated Indians, Malays or Chinese who were probably draughtsmen in European construction firms or government departments. These designers, with names like R.T. Rajoo, Tan Seng Chong, Almeida, Kassim and J.B. Westerhout, freely plagiarized western architectural motifs.

From the mid-1920s, plans were drawn up and submitted by British architects. For a while, the plasterwork became more robust before it disappeared altogether. The wide use of reinforced concrete, instead of timber lintels and loadbearing walls, saw the gradual disappearance of some vernacular elements like verandah roofs and roof terrace balusters.

R. IAN LLOYD

IAN C. STEWART

LEFT AND ABOVE: The V-shaped Jinrikisha building (1903) provides a strong visual anchor at the junction of Tanjong Pagar Road, Neil Road and South Bridge Road. Although only two storeys high, the strategically placed dome and Classical details of the facade (including a fine broken pediment within the arched pediment) lend an unusual dignity and presence which goes beyond the building's actual dimensions. The first jinrikishas arrived from Shanghai in 1880 and in 1892 a special ordinance was passed to look after the vehicles in response to their uncontrolled growth. They were replaced by trishaws in 1946-47. Today the building is a Maternal and Child Care Centre.

Three views of Keong Saik Street. The street runs in a broad sweep from New Bridge Road (below) and is linked continuously with many buildings of interest. The five-foot way (far right) with red painted pintu pagar has original tiles. The red brick building (right) is a mix of Modern and Classical elements.

R. IAN LLOYD

R. IAN LLOYD

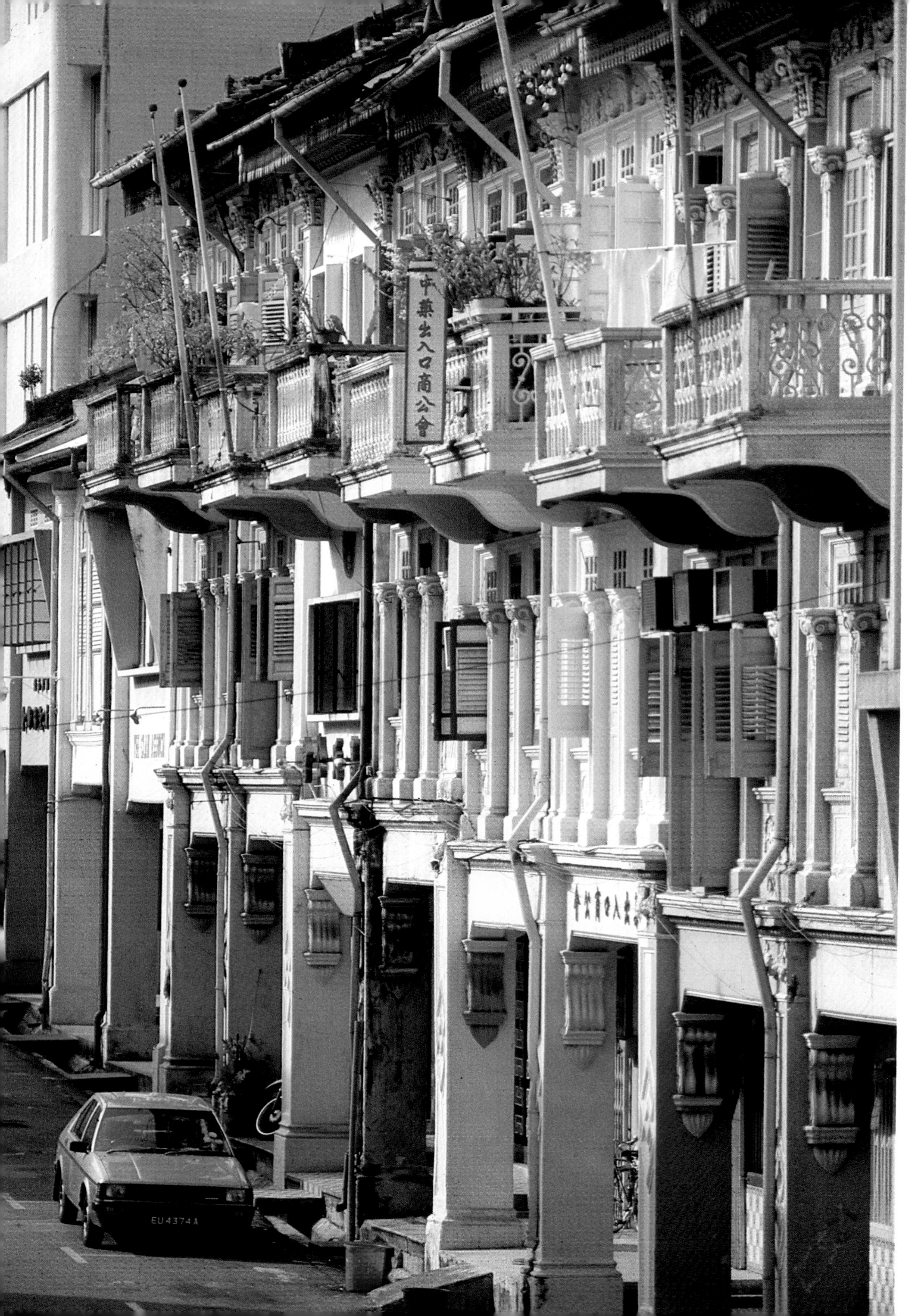

R. IAN LLOYD

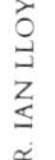

R. IAN LLOYD

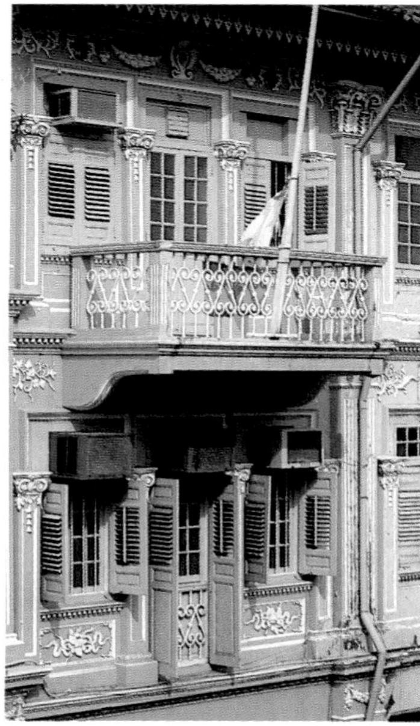

LEFT: The balconies of Bukit Pasoh. Built between 1933 and 1937, this grouping of eight terraces stepping up the street is particularly flamboyant, with cantilevered balconies, iron lace balustrades, carved timber fascia boards (all intact) and Renaissance-style decorative plasterwork.

R. IAN LLOYD

R. IAN LLOYD

RIGHT: No 31 to 37 Bukit Pasoh, originally built as four dwelling units in 1927 by architect W. T. Foo. The facades are relatively plain but with beautiful stained glass fanlights. The cantilevered balconies have green Chinese porcelain roof tiles and the centre panels have "fish scale" balustrades.

Duxton Plain Parkway was once a railway reserve. It runs under Neil Road from Yan Kit Swimming Complex to New Bridge Road and was established before World War II. Today it remains a delightful shady green relief in the heart of the city.

R. IAN LLOYD

1 *Blair Road*
2 *Spottiswoode Park Road*
3 *Neil Road*
4 *New Bridge Road*

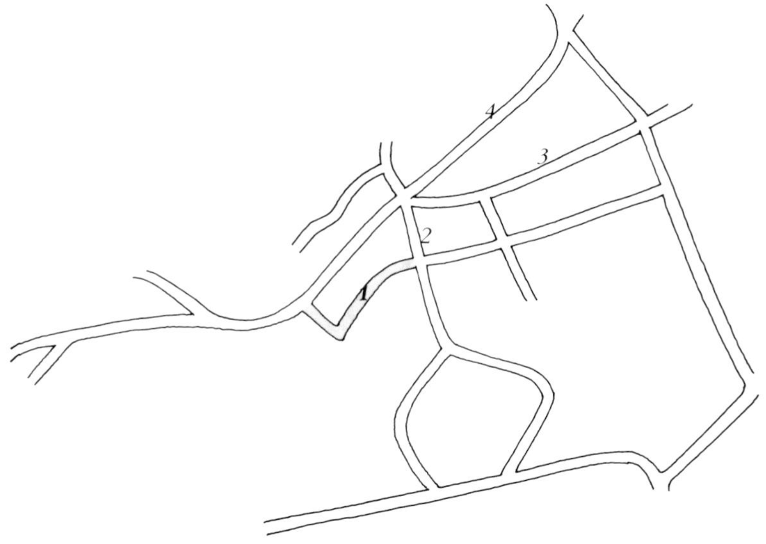

BLAIR ROAD

KOUO SHANG-WEI

The entrance to Blair Road.

The elaborate examples of Straits Chinese residential terrace houses along Blair Road were built in the 1920s as part of the general expansion of the town. Blair Road was laid in 1900 and is named after John Blair, a senior official of the Tanjong Pagar Dock Company in the 1880s. Spottiswoode Park gets its name from the Spottiswoode family who ran an early merchant firm set up in 1824.

The uniqueness of terrace houses such as these is largely due to the fact that they are an eclectic mixture of Chinese, Malay, European and Colonial elements.

The distinctive Chinese character is given by the courtyard plan of the house interior and by the rounded gable ends of the pitched roofs. The small verandah overhangs, which are roofed with green porcelain Chinese bamboo-shaped tiles, are distinctly Chinese as are the granite corbels which support them. On some of the older buildings the bases of the first storey columns are carved out of solid granite imported from China. Granite was also used for verandah floor edgings.

Other Chinese features include the red, curved clay tiles, or pantiles, of the main roof; the fan-shaped or bat-wing-shaped air vents above the first storey windows; the green ceramic balusters used for roof balustrades and, in some of the older houses, friezes of coloured ceramic chips depicting dragons, phoenixes and flowers. The Malay influence comes in the form of timber fretwork for balustrades, eaves and fascia boards.

The European influence is expressed in the louvred timber shutters brought by the British via India; the panelled main entrance doors or *pintu besar*; the French windows or Venetian windows sometimes used on the upper floors; and in the use of fanlights and in the plasterwork. The Portuguese jalousie, the shuttered windows with slats sloping upwards from outside, is another European contribution. The imprint of the early Colonial architects, surveyors and engineers can be seen in the repetition of certain ornamentation and details, such as the Corinthian pilasters on the upper storeys.

IAN C. STEWART

LEFT: Nos. 57 and 58 Spottiswoode Park Road. Two contemporaneous but non-identical three-storey terraces. No. 57 (left) has a wider facade which incorporates the five-foot way in an interesting manner. The third storey verandahs and Classical details give the air of an Italian palazzo.

BELOW: Nos. 2, 4, 6, Blair Road. The three stepped terraces with fluted Composite–style pilasters and faux circular and triangular pediments above the second storey windows follow the road curve.

RIGHT: Details reveal the richness of the Blair Road terrace houses.

KOUO SHANG-WEI

R. IAN LLOYD

Exceptionally rich plaster bas reliefs, the generous forecourts of the houses, the quiet residential ambiance of the street and the excellent condition of the buildings are features which make Blair Road something special. The five houses below, Nos. 25 to 33 on the south side of the street, are part of a continuous row of 14 houses with similar elevational treatment. The houses would have been built in groups of four or six by different owners circa the 1920s. On the north side of the street, are more houses linked by a five-foot way. Nos. 8 to 14 and Nos. 30 to 54 are more ornate with beautifully carved pintu pagar and imported tiles.

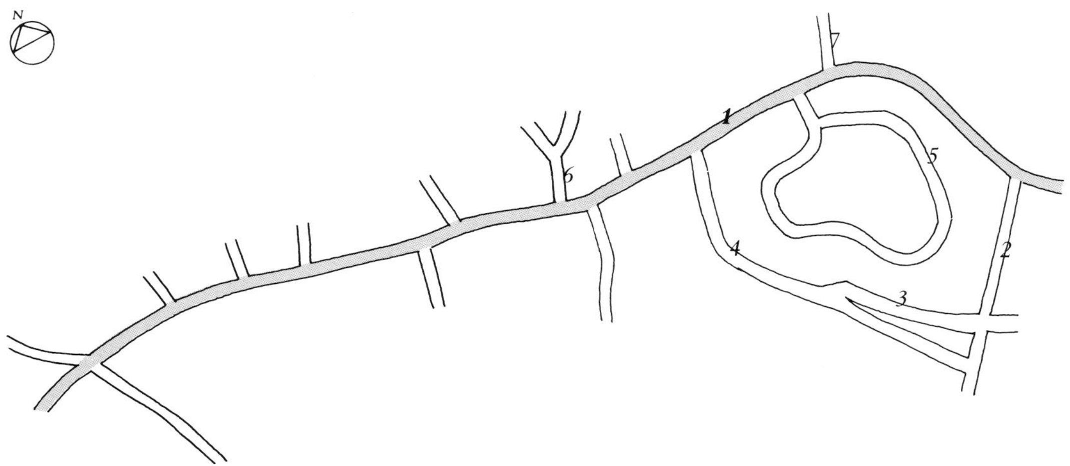

1 River Valley Road
2 Mohamed Sultan Road
3 Tong Watt Road
4 Kim Yam Road
5 Institution Hill
6 Killiney Road
7 Oxley Road

RIVER VALLEY ROAD

For many years, River Valley Road was at the outskirts of the city. The portion of the road from Hill Street to the back of Government Hill (Fort Canning) only is shown on the government map of 1836. Beyond was marshy lowland and a few drier hillocks.

It was on one of those hillocks that Baba merchant Tan Jiak Kim, grandson of Tan Kim Seng, built his suburban villa, Panglima Prang (now demolished), in the 1860s. Another settler was Lee Cheng Yan, a Malacca-born boy who moved to Singapore in 1859 and stayed in Telok Ayer Street, became wealthy and built Magenta Villa at the corner of River Valley and Killiney Road circa the 1870s. He is immortalized in Cheng Yan Place.

What occurred in River Valley during this period was part of the natural expansion of the town. By the 1860s people like Mr Tan were buying up abandoned plantations, especially in the areas nearer town, subdividing the land and building homes. River Valley, reasonably close to Boat Quay and convenient to Chinatown, was a popular area. Another wealthy merchant, Tan Yeok Nee, built his suburban home in the traditional Chinese style on Clemenceau Avenue in 1885. Today it is the only surviving example of the traditional Chinese courtyard house in Singapore. Early development of residential terrace houses took place along Mohamed Sultan Road in 1895 and in Tong Watt Road in 1897.

All the families who moved to this area probably had lived in the central area of the town. The move outward was linked to increased family prosperity and growing family size. It also coincided with the period when the Straits Chinese reaching the height of their power and position of influence. House plans were related to the social customs of the day, when large families — including several wives, in-laws, children and servants — living together under one roof was the norm.

"The roads leading from one to another of these residences, and from them to the town, are very pleasant walks or drives, according as it may be morning or evening. Of those leading into and out of town, Orchard Road and River Valley Road are the two chief. The former is the approach to the greater number of houses, and has the most traffic; it is, besides, probably the prettier of the two. Shortly after leaving town, it follows the windings of a small stream of anything but pellucid water, in which the dhobies, or washermen, are busy from morning till night, on Sabbaths and on weekdays . . . beating away at the soiled lined of the clothed section of the population."

– John Cameron, Our Tropical Possessions in Malayan India (1865).

R. IAN LLOYD

ABOVE: Stepped-up terraces at the corner of River Valley and Kim Yam Roads.

RIGHT: House, No 279 River Valley Road. There are still many such early 20th century two-storey houses dotting the River Valley area. Arranged on a symmetrical plan with a front portico and verandah, high ceilings and servants quarters separated from the main body of the house, these buildings feature a combination of European Classical, Chinese and Malay elements.

R. IAN LLOYD

R. IAN LLOYD

IAN C. STEWART

Early examples of Singapore Eclectic architecture, Nos 1–7 Tong Watt Street (also on the cover). The row of seven contiguous terrace houses abuts a row of five with more pronounced Chinese influences. Until the advent of concrete in Singapore, the length of felled timber available determined the width of the shophouses. No. 1 (above) has an unusual medallion in the entablature featuring a pair of chimera. The fan light windows, a feature of so many Classical buildings, first appeared in Europe as a rectangular transom window over early 18th century entry doors. Designed to allow light into the entry vestibule, the early fanlights often had bars of wood arranged in geometric patterns — including radiating bars resembling a fan. In the tropical climate fanlights proved a useful way of allowing in light, especially when used together with Portuguese jalousies, as here. Later building saw the replacement of glass fanlights with Malay-inspired carved timber panels.

Two facades from Mohamed Sultan Road. The three-storey terrace houses along the road are more Chinese in character and include fine examples of Chinese geometric carved timber panels, painted scrolls and pintu pagar. The windows are part of a grouping of six contiguous but different terrace houses with elaborate handcrafted details now in disrepair. No 9, one of a grouping of seven further up the road, also has some fine woodwork in the interior.

Painted scrolls above first-storey windows on Tong Watt Street. The colours remain vivid nearly a century after their painting.

Interior of No 27 Mohamed Sultan Road. The dado along the front room walls is still evident. The timber frame separating the front room would once have held an elaborately carved screen. The airwell, a feature of many deep shophouses or residential terraces, has a floor several centimetres lower than the red "Malacca" floor tiles and is edged in granite. The airwell includes an altar-like construction (bottom) and Chinese friezes grace its walls.

IAN C. STEWART

IAN C. STEWART

R. IAN LLOYD

R. IAN LLOYD

IAN C. STEWART

R. IAN LLOYD

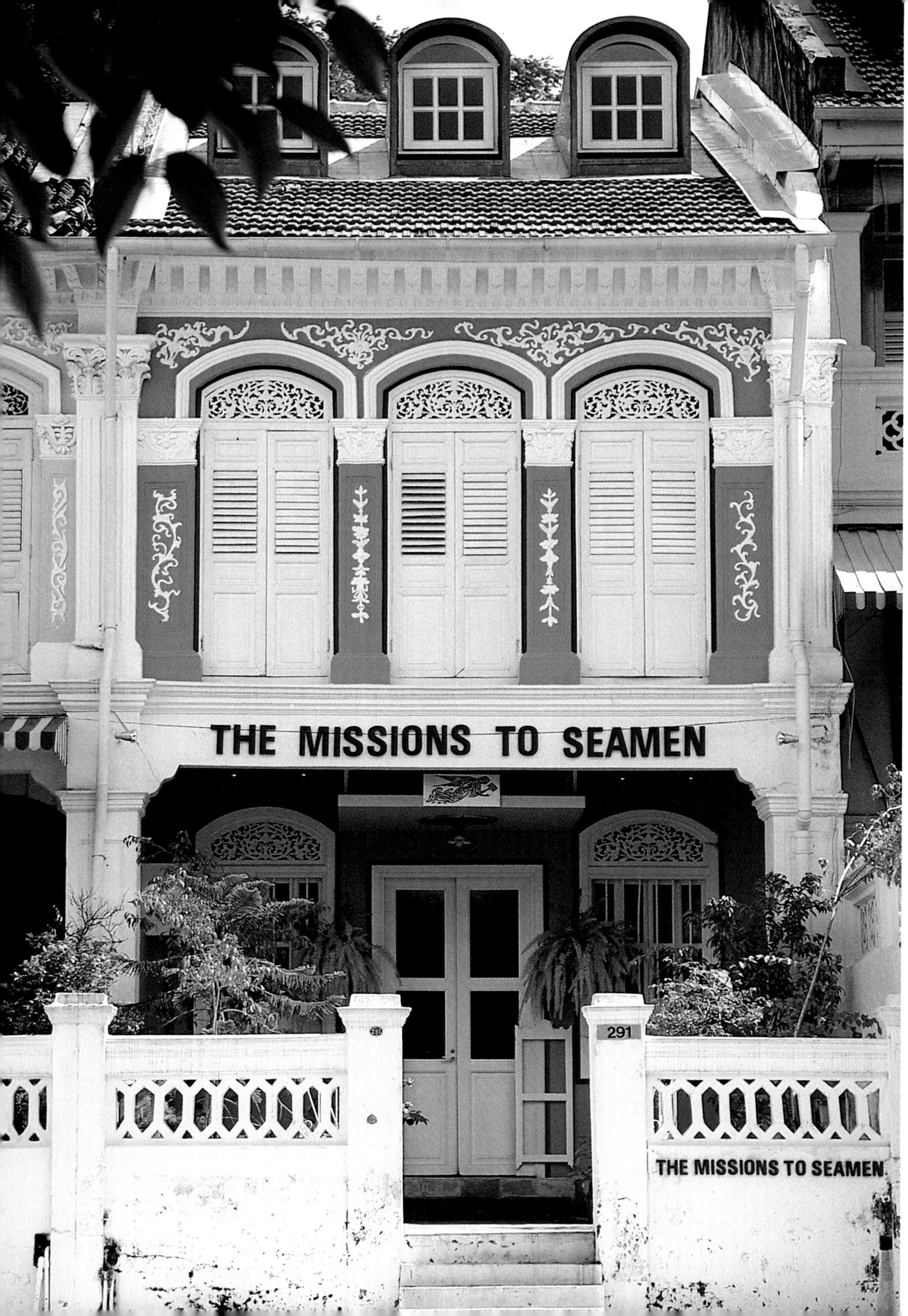

R. IAN LLOYD

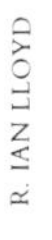

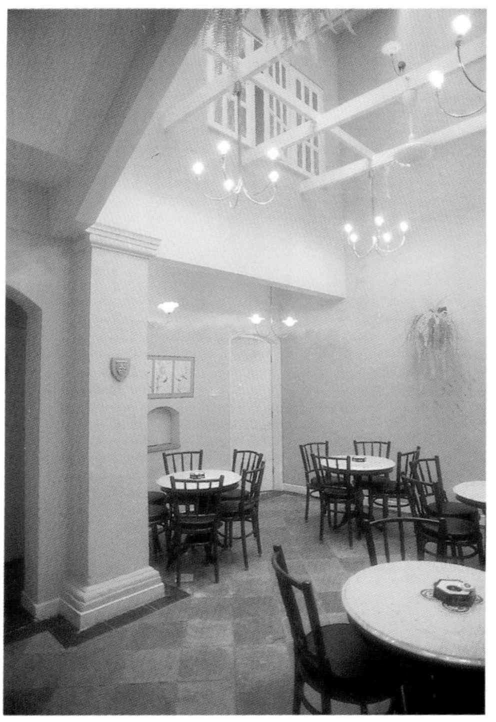

R. IAN LLOYD

LEFT: The Missions to Seamen, No. 291 River Valley Road. A renovation was undertaken in the spirit of preservation and efforts were made to enhance the historical quality of the building. Practical needs were met by the addition at the back of a second storey and a skylight to give internal light.

ABOVE: The interior.

1 Beach Road
2 Jalan Sultan
3 Victoria Street
4 Rochor Road
5 Aliwal Street
6 Pahang Street
7 Baghdad Street
8 Kandahar Street
9 Bussorah Street
10 Muscat Street
11 Sultan Mosque
12 Sultan Gate
13 North Bridge Road
14 Middle Road
15 Liang Seah Street
16 Purvis Street

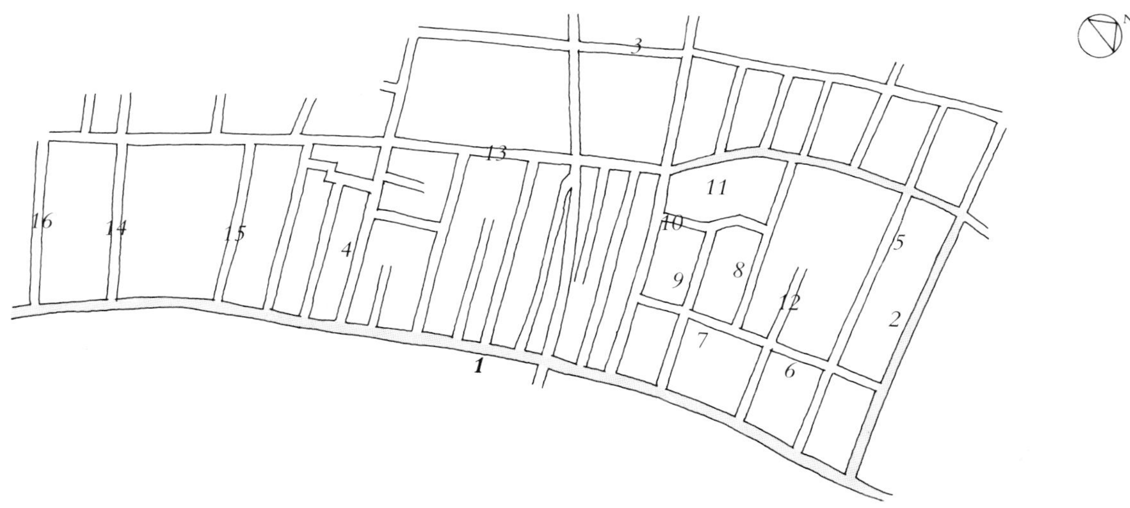

KAMPONG GLAM

"There is a story about how Mr. Raffles and Colonel Farquhar together debated the best way to enlarge the Settlement. Colonel Farquhar considered that Kampong Glam should become the business quarter, that is to say a trading centre with markets and so forth. But Mr. Raffles thought that the business quarter should be on the near side of the river. Colonel Farquhar said "This side is very unsuitable as the ground is all muddy and the water is not good. It will be very costly to reclaim the land. Besides, where can we obtain sufficient earth for banking?" Mr. Raffles replied "If Kampong Glam were to become a business area this side of the river would remain unimproved for as long as a hundred years." Each of the two men held firmly to his own opinion, the one saying this the other that, each trying to find support for his view. They thought the matter over for three days. Then it occurred to Mr. Raffles that the small hill near Tanjong Singapura might be broken up and the earth used for banking on the near side of the river. The next day the two of them considered this idea and agreed to it."

– Munshi Abdullah, The Founding of Singapore, translated by A.H. Hill in The Malaysian Branch of the Royal Asiatic Society: Singapore 150 Years.

Like Chinatown and Serangoon Road, Kampong Glam owes its significance as much to its history and ethnic flavour as to the pleasing quality of its streetscapes and architecture.

Its origins date back to the granting of a large tract of land to Sultan Hussein Shah in 1823 measuring 22.9 ha "to the east of the European town and lying between Rochor River and the sea, measuring in front along Beach Road 731 feet, at back of Chuliah Kampong and along Rochor River about 1,200 feet, in depth from Beach Road to Rochor River about 2,100 feet." The name Kampong Glam comes from the Glam trees which once grew in the area. The trees provided a medicinal oil and the bark was used by the Bugis and the Malays to caulk their boats.

As had occurred with the Padang, Raffles had an argument with the first resident, Col. William Farquhar, over the future of Kampong Glam. Farquhar had envisaged the business quarter centred there, but Raffles favoured the Singapore River's south side, reasoning "If Kampong Glam were to become a business area, this side of the river would remain unimproved for as long as a hundred years."

But develop it did as Bugis, Arabs, Javanese, Boyanese and other Muslims settled around Sultan Hussein Shah's enclave. In the late 1820s convict labourers drained 11.4 ha of mangrove swamp at Kampong Glam and intersected it with roads of covered gutters so that by January, 1831 one-fifth of the land had good upper-roomed houses built on it. Streets like Arab, Bussorah, Baghdad, Muscat and Jalan Sultan were laid out at this time.

The Sultan replaced his large wood and attap Istana with a handsome Palladian house sometime between 1836 and 1843. There is some speculation that the building, which still stands, was designed by G.D. Coleman. If not, it certainly shows his influence. The first Sultan Mosque was constructed in 1825. Nearby, along Beach Road, a wealthy Malacca-born lady, Hajjah Fatimah, erected a mosque in 1846 which bears her name.

The western boundary of Kampong Glam formed the European town. Until the 1880s, Beach Road was the fashionable residential neighbourhood. One of the Chinese names for Beach Road is still "20 House Street", deriving from the row of 20 elegant villas which stood well back from the road in large compounds with gardens in front and verandahs painted green. Singapore pioneer Dr Jose d'Almeida built the last house in the row in 1825. The home of this Portuguese medical practitioner, merchant and agriculturalist became the centre of the settlement's more privileged social life.

Today the main pre-war building form in the Kampong Glam area is the two-and three-storey shophouse. There is a predominance of plainer, humble, utilitarian structures interspersed with those that have a Palladian or Baroque influence, such as those along Bussorah Street. These buildings do not have a dramatic history, but for generations they have been an essential backdrop to everyday life.

IAN C. STEWART

LEFT: The Istana Kampong Glam was built circa 1840 and there is some speculation that it is the work of G.D. Coleman. If not, it certainly shows his influence. From this view the symmetry of the house and its simple Palladian features are clearly evident.

LEFT BELOW: Minaret and red tiled roof, a portrait of Kampong Glam.

BELOW: No. 52 Kandahar Street is one of six refulgent two-storey terrace houses with an unusual treatment of the second storey pilasters and florid "Renaissance" decorative plasterwork.

R. IAN LLOYD

R. IAN LLOYD

Two views of the west side of Bussorah Street. The 13 houses were built in groupings of five, three and two and are still painted in the favoured pastel shades. The row of two-storey terraces opposite are of the plain, simpler variety.

R. IAN LLOYD

BELOW: *No. 97 Ling Seah Street, one of a pair of four storey buildings capped with a small tower. The repeated use of painted chick blinds gives the building added texture. The partner of this building has been demolished.*

BOTTOM: *No. 321 Sultan Gate is a more modern version of shophouse architecture.*

RIGHT ABOVE: *No. 62 and 64 Aliwal Street, two of five houses which face an equally attractive row of seven.*

RIGHT: *No. 14 Pahang Street, one of four units at the junction of Pahang Street and Aliwal Street.*

R. IAN LLOYD

IAN C. STEWART

IAN C. STEWART

R. IAN LLOYD

R. IAN LLOYD

LEFT: No. 37 Purvis Street, a simple Palladian inspired structure with fanlights, door height timber shutters and a handsome ground floor colonnade with keystone arches. The storeys are clearly demarcated by the simple mouldings on the cornices. An exceptionally elegant and dignified structure.

ABOVE: The distinctive columns of North Bridge Road.

1 Stamford Road
2 Bras Basah Road
3 St Andrew's Cathedral
4 Armenian Street
5 Queen Street
6 Victoria Street
7 Convent of the Holy Infant Jesus
8 North Bridge Road
9 St Joseph's Institution
10 Cathedral of the Good Shephend
11 Raffles City

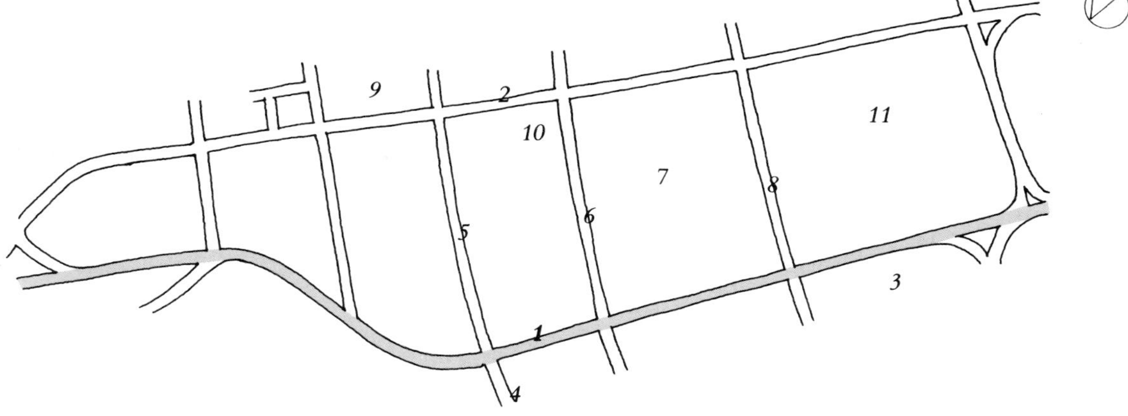

STAMFORD ROAD

IAN C. STEWART

The green field unifying Stamford and Bras Basah Roads framed here by two 19th century domed roofs: St Joseph's Institution (1867) in the foreground and the National Museum (1886–87) in the background.

Stamford Road is an important environmental area not only because of the pleasing buildings along the street, but because of the green lung stretching from the Cathay Building towards the sea that separates it from its sister street, Bras Basah Road.

Stamford Road was constructed in 1823 and takes its name from Singapore's founder. Bras Basah is Malay for wet rice, presumably because wet rice was left to dry in the sun beside the Sungei Bras Basah, now Stamford Canal.

The buildings which are in Stamford Road today reflect one facet of Singapore's urban richness: the diversity of Colonial architecture. From the English Gothic St Andrew's Cathedral (1862), designed by Ronald MacPherson, Executive Engineer and Superintendent of the Public Works Department, to the Victorian style National Museum, designed and built by the Public Works Department in 1886, with subsequent extensions in 1906, 1916 and 1926.

In between, there is Shaws Building, a 1930s addition to the streetscape designed by Keys and Dowdeswell in the rather ponderous Neo-Classical style. Stamford House, a familiar site on the road since its completion in 1914, was designed by Swan and Maclaren for Whiteaway Laidlaw and Co and clearly shows evidence of Bidwell's deft hand. Nearby is the MPH Building which was designed for the Methodist Publishing House in 1908 and is a good example of the Edwardian architecture so popular in England circa 1900.

The area was traditionally the location of churches and schools. In addition to the Convent of the Holy Infant Jesus and St Joseph's Institution (see pages *78* and *135*) there is the simple yet dignified Cathedral of the Good Shepherd which opened its doors to worshippers in 1843. It was designed by another early architect, Denis McSwiney, and is gazetted as a national monument. A modern monumental addition to the streetscape is Raffles City, designed by famous New York-based architect I.M. Pei on the original site of Raffles Institution.

R. IAN LLOYD

LEFT: *Despite the diversity of architectural styles of different periods, this stretch of Stamford Road has an amazing degree of coherence achieved through two features common to the buildings: They are of uniform heights and their designers showed good manners in relating the buildings to the street and the surrounding buildings.*

BELOW: *Shaws Building (1930) was designed by two British architects named Keys and Dowdeswell who came to Singapore in the 1920s to execute several government projects, including Singapore General Hospital and the Fullerton Building. Among their private commissions: The Heeron Building on Orchard Road and Shaws Building. All of these share the heavy, rather ponderous Neo-Classical style then fashionable.*

IAN C. STEWART

KOUO SHANG-WEI

ABOVE AND RIGHT: Stamford House (1904) was designed by Swan and Maclaren at a time when R.A.J. Bidwell exerted a strong influence on the firm. It has a Classical, symmetrical composition with a central raised curved pediment and triangular pediments at the ends. Other Classical elements include the keystone arches and the second storey Venetian windows. The richly decorated roof balustrade and the exuberant entablatures which divide the storeys further enhance the facade.

IAN C. STEWART

LEFT: Another view of Stamford Road.

BELOW: This later more modern (1930s) addition to Stamford Road retained many of the characteristics of earlier shophouse architecture including the five foot way, the narrow frontage of the individual units, the window treatment and the way the building turns the corner. The corner is given additional definition by the raised roof with Chinese inspired bracket details.

RIGHT: The MPH building (1908) has repetitive curved pediments as a decorative element on top of the building and on top of each of the windows.

BELOW: Tao Nan School (1910). The school was started in 1906 and was one of the half dozen early Chinese schools here. The interior of this three-storey eclectic building was destroyed by the Japanese in World War II and rebuilt in 1945. The school moved to new premises in Marine Parade in 1983.

KOUO SHANG-WEI

R. IAN LLOYD

R. IAN LLOYD

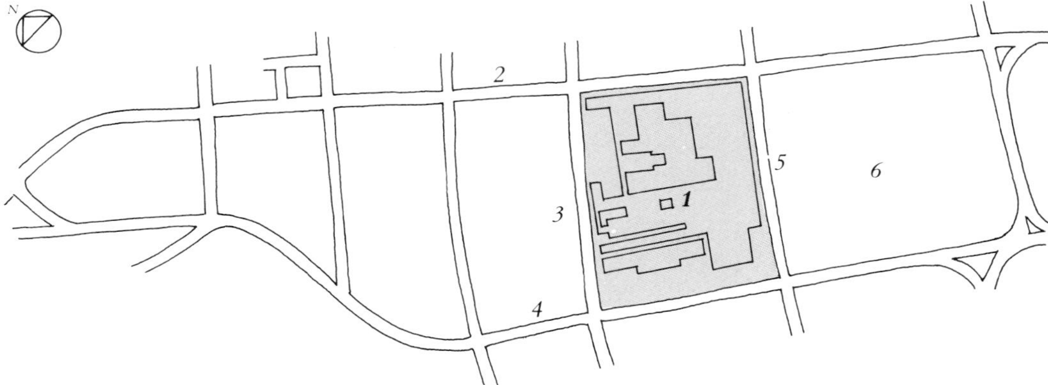

1 Convent of the Holy Infant Jesus
2 Bras Basah Road
3 Victoria Street
4 Stamford Road
5 North Bridge Road
6 Raffles City

THE CONVENT OF THE HOLY INFANT JESUS

The Convent is almost a town in itself. The thick walls and massive gates around the perimeter of a city block enclose a unique group of buildings which span 140 years of Singapore's architectural history set around serene green spaces.

The oldest building in the area was the private residence of Mr H.C. Caldwell, a government clerk. It was designed by G.D. Coleman and erected in 1840-41. In 1852, the house was purchased by the dynamic French Catholic priest Father Beurel along with six other houses on the site for the establishment of a convent school. In 1854, the first group of four nuns arrived and quickly set about their teaching activities. For many years the downstairs of the Caldwell house was the Convent parlour and visitors' room, while the upstairs room, with its semi-circular shape, was a recreation room for the nuns. Here they did their sewing, reading and writing.

The grounds were expanded and new buildings constructed as funds allowed. In 1863, more land between Victoria Street and North Bridge Road was purchased from Raffles Institution. Then, in 1890, the school was given a boost when the French Gothic-style chapel with its beautiful stained glass windows and several additional buildings were constructed, designed by the French priest-architect Father Nain who also designed the curved wings of St Joseph's Institution.

In 1913, another building was constructed which later became the premises of St Nicholas Girls' School. The school itself was established in 1933 and first held classes in the four old Hotel Van Wijk bungalows which had been built on the Stamford Road side in the 1890s and were later incorporated into the convent's grounds. The latest addition is the building designed by Swan and Maclaren, circa 1950, on the Stamford Road side.

In December 1983, the school closed the massive doors for the last time and moved to a new location in Toa Payoh.

IAN C. STEWART

ABOVE: What makes the Convent such an important element of the city is not only the architectural quality of its buildings, but the peaceful cloister-like grounds between them.

RIGHT: The lush greenery in the Convent's grounds frames the Gothic Revival chapel and adjacent buildings constructed in the 1890s. Especially attractive: the courtyard spaces created by the covered walkways and the cloister-like atmosphere.

IAN C. STEWART

RIGHT: *A generous link in the Convent grounds. Note the stubby Doric-style columns, the supporting timber trussed roof, the red roof tiles and the large terra-cotta floor tiles.*

BELOW: *Interior of the Caldwell House. Built in 1841, the house became part of the Convent in 1852. It was designed by G.D. Coleman and has an unusual semi-circular front abutting the main rectangular block. Note the Classical details, such as the dentils along the edge of the ceiling and the Ionic columns in the foreground. The original timber-louvred windows and doors have been replaced by adjustable glass louvres. This room long served as the private sitting room of the teaching sisters.*

RIGHT: Interior of the Convent chapel looking towards the apse. Note the vaulted ceiling clustered columns and pointed arches so typical of Gothic and Gothic Revival buildings.

BELOW: A view from the rear balcony.

IAN C. STEWART

IAN C. STEWART

OVERLEAF: The stained glass windows of the chapel.

1 Serangoon Road
2 Owen Road
3 Race Course Road
4 Roberts Lane
5 Burmah Road
6 Rangoon Road

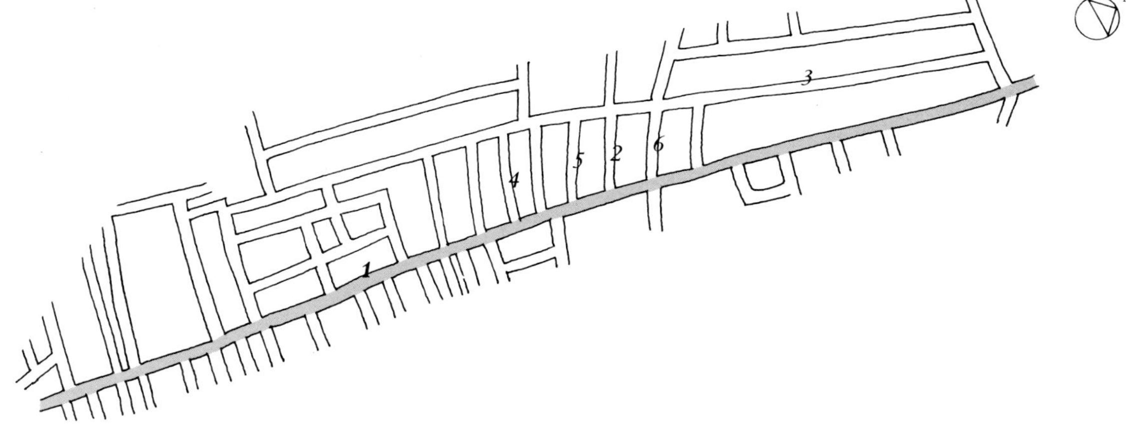

SERANGOON ROAD

"We began our journey through the space and time of Serangoon Road in order to arrive at an understanding of its role in the context of the Indian community in Singapore. As it is with most such journeys, we encountered more than we bargained for. One restaurant proprietor described the areas as an "every-kind-of-people-coming-place", and indeed it is. A sari shop salesman labelled it as a "Second Madras" and in a way this is also true. All in all, however, the area is Singaporean – evolving initially as an integral part of the 19th century colonial world and later moulded by the rapid developments occurring in this city-state during the post-independence period. The area is a relic of the past, a vital part of the present, and a question mark for the future."

– Sharon Siddique and Nirmala Puru Shotam, Singapore's Little India, Past, Present and Future (1983).

Serangoon Road, Singapore's "Little India", cannot be discussed only in architectural terms, although many of the roads in the area contain fine examples of Singapore Eclectic Architecture. Its importance to the city is also due to its unique ethnic character and, like Chinatown or Kampong Glam, its place in history.

Unlike Chinatown or Kampong Glam, which were both designated ethnic preserves from 1822, Serangoon Road evolved. It was first an area for Indians engaged in cattle-related activities because of an abundance of water and grass. An additional factor may have been the location of the Indian convict jail on Bras Basah Road near the Dhoby Ghaut junction.

Between the 1830s and 1880s, the area, although not densely populated, embraced the interests of the highest strata of colonial society as well as the livelihood of the lowest. The Racecourse and houses of European and Eurasian civil servants co-existed with vegetable gardens, cattle pens and slaughterhouses. From the 1880s, Serangoon Road also attracted South Indian commercial settlers and eventually it became one of the four strongholds of the Indian community, along with High Street, Market and Chulia Streets and the Tanjong Pagar and Keppel Road areas.

The last two decades of the 19th century saw a large influx of population to the area. In the early 20th century, the predominance of Indian settlers is exhibited by the fact that among the building plans submitted for approval during the first decade, 10 were of Chinese origin, 4 European/Eurasian and 27 of Indian ethnic origin. During these years the Eurasian and European homes which had stretched along the perimeter of the road were gradually demolished to make way for building types regarded as more suitable to the commercial character of the area. Cattle were gazetted out of the municipality in 1936. By this time, the face of Serangoon Road was much the same as today.

R. IAN LLOYD

Three of the many faces of the Serangoon Road area. The turquoise building along Owen Road (left) has delicate plaster mouldings as does the wall surrounding the house at the corner of Race Course and Rangoon Roads (below). The house is one of the few bungalows still standing in what was once a popular residential area. Many of the roads emanating from Serangoon Road, in fact, started as private access roads to individual houses. The laundry, No 279 Serangoon Road (bottom) is reminiscent of Victorian England with its cast iron columns and upper storey bay window.

R. IAN LLOYD

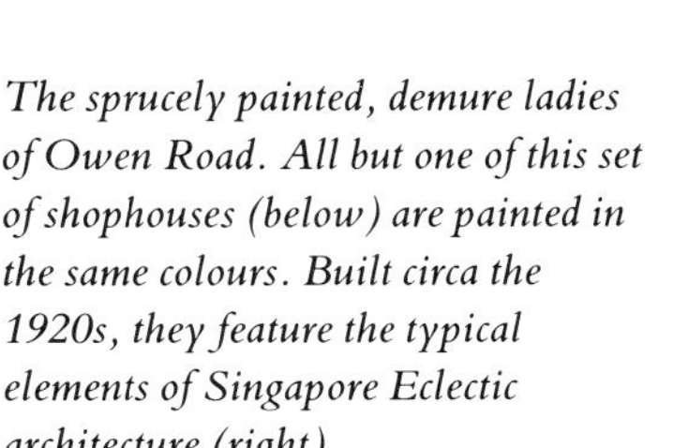

The sprucely painted, demure ladies of Owen Road. All but one of this set of shophouses (below) are painted in the same colours. Built circa the 1920s, they feature the typical elements of Singapore Eclectic architecture (right).

R. IAN LLOYD

R. IAN LLOYD

R. IAN LLOYD

Two sets of residential terrace houses on Roberts Lane. The six units in the foreground (left) are baroque pastel portraits, complete with European tiles, timber casement windows, elaborate plasterwork mouldings, Classical inspired details and cantilevered balconies. The eight more "modern" terrace houses (details below) are a distinctly different expression of shophouse architecture yet certain features have been retained such as the timber casement windows, the cantilevered upper storeys and the European tiles.

R. IAN LLOYD

RIGHT: More beauties along Roberts Lane. There is an enormous variety in the modulations of the Singapore Eclectic style as this ornate pair illustrate once again. Although facade details are indicated on many of the early building plans, it was probably the imagination, skill and personal interpretation of the craftsmen involved in the implementation which accounts for the fact that virtually no two sets of shophouses are exactly alike.

R. IAN LLOYD

ABOVE: Scenes such as these with human figures are rarely found among the many glazed, patterned decorative tiles. Floral and animal motifs or geometric patterns are much more common.

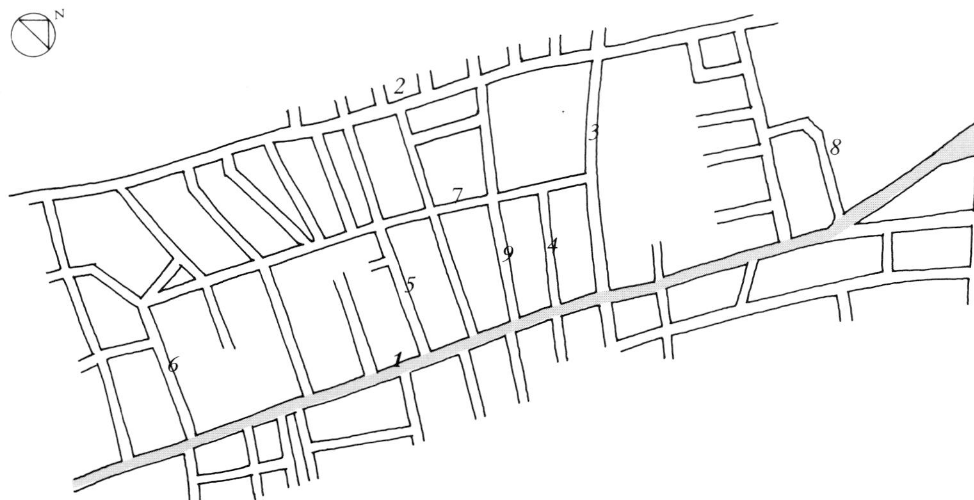

1 *Jalan Besar*
2 *Serangoon Road*
3 *Syed Alwi Road*
4 *Desker Road*
5 *Veerasamy Road*
6 *Upper Weld Road*
7 *Kampong Kapor Road*
8 *Petain Road*
9 *Rowell Road*

JALAN BESAR

Jalan Besar and the roads which link it with Serangoon Road contain many fine examples of Singapore Eclectic architecture at its most robust. Fortunately, many of these streets remain intact.

During the late 19th century only two roads bisected the area: Dunlop Street, closer to the heavily-built-up and densely populated Sungei Road area, and Syed Alwi Road, named after a descendant of Syed Omar Al Junied, founder of the Malacca Mosque, Singapore's oldest. Syed Alwi Road crossed swampy terrain and separated Chinese vegetable gardens, towards Lavender Street, from Kampong Kapor. Kampong Kapor was originally settled by many Bawaenese syces and horse trainers who worked at the Racecourse and they were joined by other Indian Muslim settlers.

In the early 20th century Kampong Kapor was drained, marking the beginning of the rapid urbanisation of the area. Roads such as Rowell, Desker, Upper Weld and Mayo, Veerasamy and Norris were laid out across the filled land and a flurry of building activity followed.

Most of the historic buildings in this area are still painted in the favoured pastel colours of pink, green, blue, beige or yellow — truly pastel portraits of Singapore's architectural heritage. Colour originally played an important role in the treatment of the facade and was carefully selected for its symbolic value. Green, for example, represents Spring and is a sign of permanency and peace. Pink, another favoured colour, is a sign of good fortune and happiness.

R. IAN LLOYD

Jalan Besar is an area particularly rich in the vernacular architecture of the 1920s as this unique row of nine shophouses on Syed Alwi Road illustrates. Because of the streets which cross it, Jalan Besar has strong links with Serangoon Road.

BELOW AND RIGHT: *The baroque facades of Nos. 61–69 Syed Alwi Road feature richly decorated Composite pilasters and oval-shaped windows (similar to ones at Victoria Memorial Hall) surrounded by bas-relief festoon mouldings. The robust yet delicate plasterwork is among the best in Singapore.*

R. IAN LLOYD

More treasures along Syed Alwi Road. The two shophouses Nos. 77–78 are a celebration of ornamentation — From the florid cornice, the "egg and dart" moulding and the dentil course of the window architraves, to the elaborate capitals of the pilasters, the wreaths or festoons surrounding the air vents, the timber fretwork of the eaves' fascia and the rich use of European tiles.

R. IAN LLOYD

Flamboyant twins, these three-storey shophouses at the junction of Veerasamy Road and Jalan Besar form a pleasant visual contrast to the modern Rowell Court housing estate behind. Both building types are unique to Singapore (Singapore Eclectic and Housing and Development Board) and together they serve as a visual reminder of the generations who have left their imprint on the city. Details of the balconies (right) show the rich combination of colour, form and decoration.

R. IAN LLOYD

R. IAN LLOYD

BELOW: *The shady junction of Kampong Kapor and Rowell Road.*

R. IAN LLOYD

R. IAN LLOYD

ABOVE AND RIGHT: *Desker Road. These very fine examples of Singapore Eclectic architecture were built between 1900 and 1910 and are painted in shades of sky-blue, baby-blue, jade green and apple green — colours reminiscent of the finely stitched kebayas once worn by Nonyas. The panels of the first storey timber window shutters have been painted so as to accentuate the carving (right). The shutters open to reveal an ornate balustrade (above right). Such balustrades were either made from timber or cast iron balusters.*

R. IAN LLOYD

R. IAN LLOYD

R. IAN LLOYD

A colourful streetscape along Upper Weld Road, a short angled road between Dickson Road and Jalan Besar, is created by the grouping of about 20 shophouses of refined design (three views shown here). The elements of the Singapore Eclectic or Chinese Baroque style are to be seen in the Chinese roof tiles, the Nonya-inspired colours, the Malay fretted timber of the eaves' fascia and the Classical elements such as the modified Corinthian or Composite columns and pilasters and the European tiles.

IAN C. STEWART

IAN C. STEWART

IAN C. STEWART

1 *Petain Road*
2 *Marne Road*
3 *Flanders Square*
4 *Somme Road*
5 *Sturdee Road*
6 *Beatty Road*
7 *Foch Road*
8 *Jalan Besar*
9 *Serangoon Road*
10 *Lavender Street*

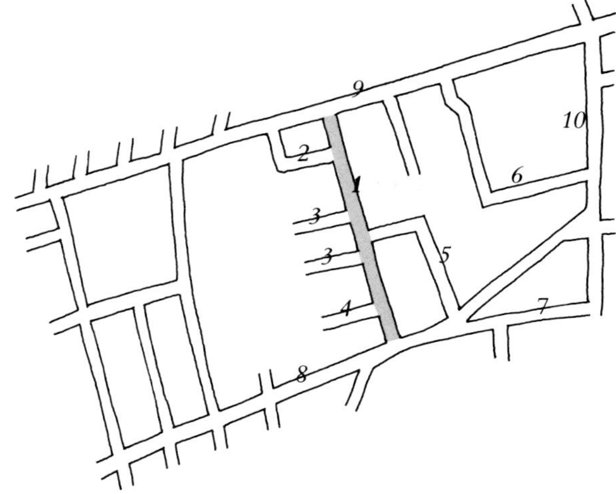

PETAIN ROAD

KOUO SHANG-WEI

No. 10 Petain Road "turns" the corner.

The stretch of 18 exceptionally rich, ornate, pastel, heavily-tiled terrace houses at No. 10 to 44 Petain Road are possibly the most homogeneous and intact group of eclectic terrace houses in Singapore.

The area developed relatively late. Until the early 20th century it was the locale for Chinese vegetable gardens. After World War I, the streets were laid out and given the names of people and places associated with famous World War I battles. Petain Road owes its name to Henri Philippe Petain (1856-1951) who was Marshal of France.

The houses were designed by J.M. Jackson, architect, civil engineer and valuer, for a certain Mohamed bin Haji Omar. Plans were submitted to the then Municipal Building Surveyors' department on 18th August 1930. During World War II, No. 10 was probably damaged by aerial bombs because, during the Occupation, plans were submitted by architect Kwan Yow Luen to the Japanese authorities in the Japanese year of 2603 (1943) for permission to carry out damage repairs.

The use of glazed ceramic tiles is particularly lavish. The colours are reminiscent of Nonya porcelain, kebayas, sarongs or beadwork. The peony flower, chrysanthemum, tulips, birds and mythical creatures predominate. The tiles were imported either from France, England, Belgium, Spain or Japan and are one of the most attractive and distinctive features of these Straits Chinese houses.

OVERLEAF: *Nos. 26 and 28, two of the 18 houses built as one unified block. This row, set back from the road with a pleasant green space in front and in excellent, intact condition, represents the full flowering of Singapore Eclectic Architecture. It is the Grand-daddy of them all. Rich, robust, and baroque, with an abundance of decoration and details that works so remarkably well – from the free use of Classical inspired orders, such as the Composite pilasters on sturdy plinths on the first storey, the second-storey Composite pilasters embellished with tiles, and the decorative plasterwork, to the Malay inspired timber fascia boards and the Chinese inspired bas relief depicting animals under the second-storey side windows. Most spectacular is the unabashedly abundant use of glazed ceramic floral tiles, primarily in green and pink colours.*

PAGE 97: *The five-foot way with original terra-cotta flooring.*

PAGE 98: *A sampler of glazed tiles from Singapore's old buildings.*

IAN C. STEWART

合境
平安

1 Emerald Hill Road
2 Saunders Road
3 Cairnhill Road
4 Clemenceau Avenue
5 Cuppage Road
6 Hullet Road
7 Orchard Road
8 Cairnhill Circle

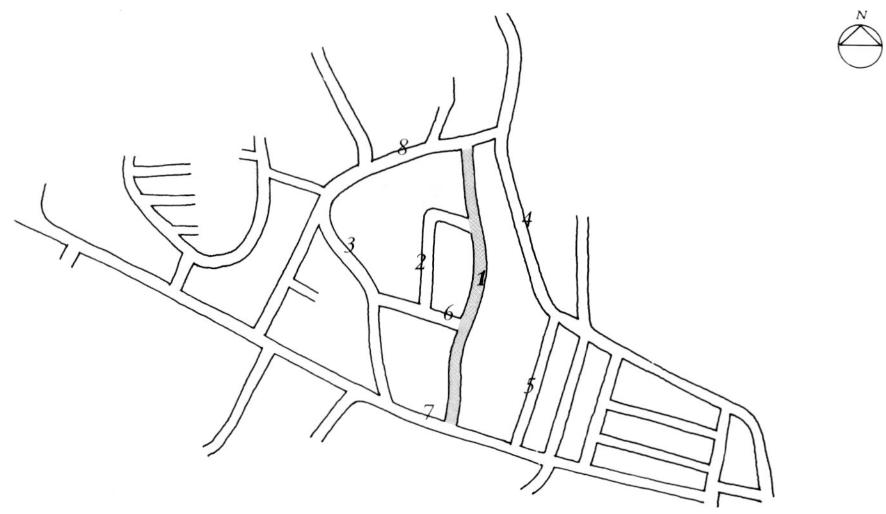

EMERALD HILL

"It is a road where tradition and history together make a brave last stand, where devil-frightener mirrors and yin-yang discs still adorn each door, where ancestors still jealously guard their altars and joss-stick holders are tacked onto every pseudo Doric pillar; a road where pigtailed amahs and sam-fooed housewives squat on the pavement gossiping or lean up against walls of tiles painted with intricate pastel flowers, ducks and pheasants..."

–Straits Times Annual 1977.

The marvellous sense of continuity along the curved, inclined Emerald Hill Road was a happy accident of history. The road was laid out in 1901 and the terrace houses were built by over 30 individual owners mostly between 1901 and 1925 at a time when good manners in architecture consisted of conforming largely to the established theme. Harmony, unity and grace are achieved by the continuous front verandahs, the common elevational treatment and the standard shophouse plan — with frontages, depths and floor heights all similar. The seemingly endless diversity comes in the rich profusion of handcrafted details.

The first legal owner of the Emerald Hill area was William Cuppage, immortalized in nearby Cuppage Road, who began his career as a postal clerk and rose to be Acting Postmaster General. Cuppage leased Emerald Hill in 1837 and received it as a permanent grant in 1845. His agricultural venture into nutmeg planting there, however, was less than successful: by the time the trees were sufficiently mature to show returns, the price of nutmegs was severely slumped and by the time the trees began to show a profit several years later, they were wiped out by disease, as were all other nutmeg plantations on the island.

Cuppage moved from his Hill Street home to Emerald Hill sometime in the early 1850s. He built two residences, Erin Lodge and Fern Cottage, living in the cottage, which was located closer to Orchard Road, until his death in 1872. The property and house were then bought by Cuppage's son-in-law, Edwin Koek, a well-known solicitor of Koek Road fame, who built another house on the property called Claregrove.

Around the turn of the century Koek encountered financial difficulties. The property passed to Thomas Rowell in 1891. Rowell sold the land and the three houses in 1900 jointly to Seah Boon Kang and Seah Eng Kiat.

It was the acquisition by the Seahs that began the transformation of Emerald Hill. In 1901, the 13.2 ha of land was subdivided into 38 plots of different sizes and sold to individuals who, in turn, carried out further subdivisions. Fern Cottage was replaced by a row of shophouses at the Orchard Road corner in 1906. Claregrove, purchased by Dr Lim Boon Keng, a leader of the Straits Chinese community, was demolished in 1924 to make way for the Singapore Chinese Girls' School and Erin Lodge was replaced by a row of shophouses backing Nos. 53 to 58 Saunders Road.

In August 1981, the Urban Redevelopment Authority designated part of the Emerald Hill area as Singapore's first area conservation scheme. The move prevented owners from altering the early 20th century facades. Already a number of houses have been renovated in a manner sympathetic to their age and character and the houses are once again becoming highly desirable residences.

BELOW LEFT: In spite of modern intrusions out of scale with the street, Emerald Hill still retains much of its historic quality, a quality enhanced by the pleasant curve of the road and the visual interest created by the repetition of the facades of approximately 150 pre-War terrace houses.

IAN C. STEWART

R. IAN LLOYD

BELOW: Nos. 39–45 Emerald Hill Road. The four terrace houses with forecourts and Chinese-style gates are an important element of the street. Interest lies in the fact that each of the three storeys has been treated differently. No. 39 (far left) is one of the many houses renovated since the 1981 announcement of Emerald Hill's status as Singapore's first conservation area.

BELOW: No 26, another terrace house sympathetically renovated. All windows and doors have been stripped of paint to reveal the beauty of the wood.

IAN C. STEWART

IAN C. STEWART

BELOW: Nos. 77, 79 and 81 further up the road share a common forecourt. The houses are part of a group of 32 built by Low Koon Yee circa 1925 along Emerald Hill and Saunders Roads. This particular grouping is in exceptionally good condition and the handcrafted details have been well maintained.

LEFT: Details of No. 67, part of the same grouping.

BELOW LEFT: *Two views of No. 98. The existing house was in a state of disrepair and had a sagging roof when the new owners purchased it in 1982. They decided, however, that as much of the existing structure and materials would be retained and reused so that not only the exterior but the interior character of the house could be preserved. All of the original exposed timber joists and floors had to be replaced (above) but the original detailing was retained. The owners had acquired a number of antique carved timber panels which have been incorporated into the building. Carved and gilded doors set on pivots (below) screen the interior from the street.*

BELOW: *An exceptionally fine door at No. 127. The house is one of five in excellent condition designed and built by the firm of Oman and Westerhout circa 1930.*

KOUO SHANG-WEI

慶祥
裕康

LEFT: Eye-catching details from the Emerald Hill houses.

No. 20 Saunders Road. One of 15 terraces with forecourts along the road, this terrace was also one of the first in the area to be renovated in a manner which enhanced the historical quality of the building. The ground floor was completely opened up, creating a voluminous expanse of space (above right). The second storey (above, far right) has an airwell while the jack roof allows for ample daylight and air circulation.

IAN C. STEWART

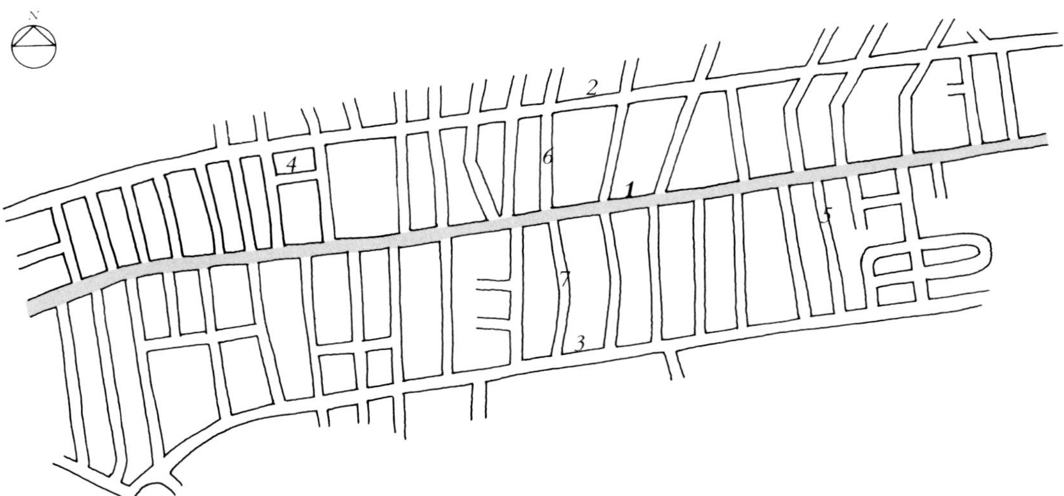

1 *Geylang Road*
2 *Sims Avenue*
3 *Guillemard Road*
4 *Lorong Bachok*
5 *Lorong 36*
6 *Lorong 27*
7 *Lorong 24A*

GEYLANG ROAD

When the suburban expansion of the town continued after World War I, Geylang became a busy thoroughfare lined with shophouses. Along the quieter lorongs, between Geylang and Sims Avenue, residential terraces and Malay-style bungalows on stilts took the place of vegetable gardens.

By now the terrace house had shrunk somewhat in size from its earlier town counterparts. But what it lacked in space, it made up for in the extravagance of its form and richness of decoration. Geylang is one of the areas where the sensitivity, skill, inventiveness and imagination of the plasterwork master craftsmen are most evident.

Traditionally the upper storeys of the terraces are more ornate than the lower ones. The riot of plasterwork decoration ranges from Renaissance motifs, like festoons and Grecian vases, to animals, baskets of fruit, flowers, English roses, Chinese mythological creatures and other whimsical figures. The entablatures are usually heavily encrusted with luxurious details.

Within the 80 years, from the 1850s to the 1930s, that the Singapore Eclectic style dominated shophouse architecture, there was such a profusion of styles and abundance of decoration as to almost defy description. The use of the classical orders on the facades, however, remained fairly consistent until the 1930s when the increasing use of structural concrete brought about the decline of their use. Houses such as these in Geylang represent the last baroque burst of handcrafted detail. The new technology, the advent of modern architecture, the changed economic and social conditions and, finally, World War II brought the demise of the Singapore Eclectic style.

Although grand architecture, both Classical and Modern, like Victoria Memorial Hall or the OCBC Centre, may be more impressive, the beautiful, surprising, even humorous and fantastic details so evident on some of Geylang's old buildings are also essential ingredients of the city, adding to its distinctive personality.

IAN C. STEWART

IAN C. STEWART

ABOVE AND RIGHT: The two faces of Geylang . . . busy commercial and quietly residential. The Geylang area is remarkably rich in Singapore Eclectic architecture. The row of 11 shophouses (top) along Geylang Road are characterised by the lavish use of tiles (detail below).

IAN C. STEWART

Part of a row of 7 houses in Lorong 35 with identical terraces, concrete balusters and spacious tiled forecourts. The interesting division of the balcony spaces allows for privacy. Similar balconies can be seen along Balestier Road and Race Course Road.

IAN C. STEWART

LEFT AND BELOW: Lorong 24A, between Sims Avenue and Guillemard Road is an unexpected delight. The two facing blocks of residential terrace houses are exquisitely Chinese Baroque. The houses feature a lavish use of ceramic tiles and Classical details, such as the pronounced "egg and dart" moulding of the first storey cornice.

R. IAN LLOYD

R. IAN LLOYD

R. IAN LLOYD

RIGHT: *A Chinese mythical animal graces one of the buildings.*

FAR RIGHT: *An unusual find: a tile frieze with a "rural" theme.*

BELOW: A building unique in all of Singapore. This rococo structure, built in 1929 at the corner of Lorong 19 and Lorong Bachok, has a main entrance flanked by Sikh guards holding rifles with bayonets. The scenic panels beneath upper storey windows (to the left) depict eclectic subjects, ranging from Chinese classical tales to a Straits soccer match and a rickshaw ride. This is certainly one of the richest examples of plasterwork in Singapore. The only other building with the honour of being watched over by Sikh guards is at the corner of Balestier Road and Jalan Kemaman. Like this Geylang cousin, it is an elaborate concoction of East and West.

RIGHT: Details from the building are an ornate feast for the eyes.

IAN C. STEWART

IAN C. STEWART

R. IAN LLOYD

House at Lorong 27, a rich example of the one-storey bungalows built in the early part of the century. The house is set on piers above the ground and follows the basic Malay house plan: a serambi, or guest verandah, in front followed by the ibu rumah, or main body of the house, and the dapor, or kitchen, at the rear. Access to the house is via two side staircases. The "Chinese baroque" ornamentation includes the timber fretwork fascia boards, the verandah balustrade, the carved timber vents above the doors as well as the delicate panels under the eaves, the unusual columns and baroque plasterwork, the European tiles and the fountain in front.

R. IAN LLOYD

R. IAN LLOYD

1 *Joo Chiat Road*
2 *Koon Seng Road*
3 *Everitt Road*
4 *Joo Chiat Lane*
5 *Joo Chiat Place*
6 *Joo Chiat Terrace*
7 *East Coast Road*

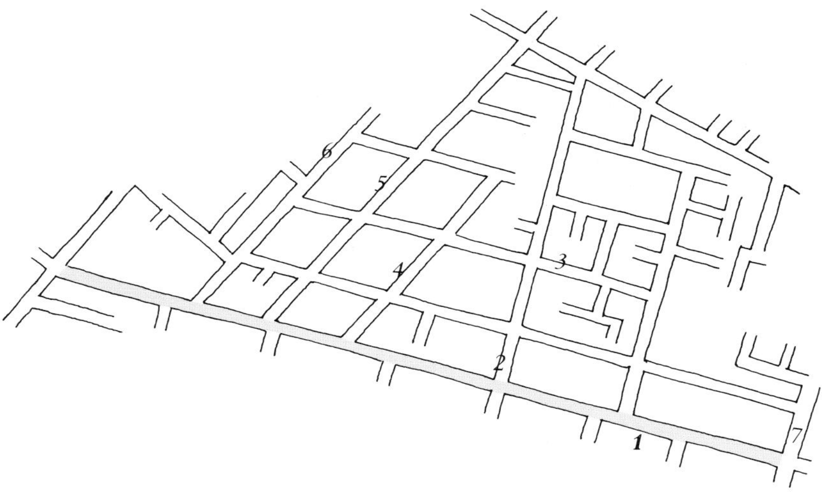

JOO CHIAT ROAD

In the early years of the century, the Joo Chiat area was planted with coconut trees as part of an estate owned by the wealthy Arabian Alsagoff family. After World War I, Chew Joo Chiat, a well-known landowner of the time, bought over a large chunk of the land. Since there were no roads, he financed their construction and later gave them to the municipality, refusing payment for them. The land was subdivided and sold and the residential terraces and shophouses were constructed in the 1920s and 1930s. Koon Seng Road was named after a Mr Cheong Koon Seng, the proprietor of a firm of auctioneers and estate agents bearing his name and still in operation today.

It is at the two rows of terrace houses facing each other along Koon Seng Road near the junction with Joo Chiat Road that the full flowering of Singapore Eclectic architecture can be seen.

On the exterior, the general visual interest or unity of all of Singapore's residential terrace houses lies in the repetition of the facade treatment. Rising from the ground level, the columns, either single or clustered, are mostly based on the Doric order. They may be either purely decorative or actually support the beam holding the upper storeys, in which case corbels, or brackets, are used. (Timber beams were used until the introduction of reinforced concrete after World War I.)

The entrance is placed centrally with windows flanking each side and consists of a pair of timber doors fronted with a fence door, or *pintu pagar*. The windows may be two or three layers. If there are three layers, the outer layer is a fixed grille of vertical iron bars, the middle layer is an opaque glass screen set in a wooden frame of one-third to one-half the window's height and the third layer is the window proper which opens inwards and consists usually of solid timber panels.

Above the windows are ventilation grilles, either separate or included within the overall frames of the windows. If included within the frame, they are usually beautifully carved timber fretwork in a square or semi-circular shape decorated with Malay or Chinese designs.

IAN C. STEWART

The pre-War terrace houses in the Joo Chiat area are, like Geylang, exceptionally ornate. This corner terrace at the junction of Joo Chiat Road and Joo Chiat Lane, dated 1928, has a pair of dragons gracing the pediment. The pediment, splayed at a 45 degree angle, gives added definition to the corner. A similar pair of pediments mark the entrance to Koon Seng Road.

On the second storey, the columns continue as flat columns or pilasters, with smaller mock pilasters on either side. The columns are capped by modified Corinthian or Composite capitals. The upper storey windows are usually in threes, although in narrow houses they are in pairs. In some of the older terrace houses one finds three French or full length windows with carved timber balustrades. The later versions combined a large central window with timber or wrought iron balustrades flanked by two smaller windows under which were placed decorated plasterwork bas-reliefs or glazed floral tiles.

Today such terrace houses can be found along many of the streets in the Joo Chiat area and even along nearby East Coast Road. Sprucely painted and well-kept, they represent the last flowering of the ornate and unique Singapore Eclectic style.

IAN C. STEWART

IAN C. STEWART

LEFT: Nos. 133 and 135 Joo Chiat Place with unusual use of verandahs on the second storeys. The ground floor squared columns are set on sturdy plinths and decorated with Composite pilasters and glazed ceramic tiles. The two houses further right, Nos. 137 and 139, are characterised by a lavish use of tiles.

ABOVE: Another house along Joo Chiat Place. This facade is one of a row of 18 contiguous terrace houses. All but one are painted in the same colour.

RIGHT: No. 229 Joo Chiat Road, one of seven contiguous terraces characterised by a lavish use of tiles, is a portrait in beige and green.

BELOW: Nos. 370–376 Joo Chiat Road, dated 1928. The trio of casement windows within each unit has replaced the more familiar combination of two half and one full windows. The octagonal bas-relief below each window, the rose medallions on each architrave, carved timber fanlights above the windows and the egg and dart moulding along the cornice of the first storey create a resplendent grouping.

IAN C. STEWART

IAN C. STEWART

IAN C. STEWART

FAR LEFT: *On Koon Seng Road, five pre-War terrace houses in excellent condition.*

LEFT: *No. 16 Koon Seng Road (foreground) marks the end of a row of terraces. The exposed side wall has a series of windows protected by sun hoods. The presence of a row of five terraces behind creates a rarely seen juxtaposition.*

BELOW: *Three of seven terrace houses Nos. 101-113 Everitt Road characterised by the use of Chinese decorative motifs in the second storey bas-reliefs.*

RIGHT: *Four richly moulded faces of Joo Chiat. Mouldings are an architectural device which work together with the light and shade they produce to give definition to the lines of a building. Thus the delicacy of moulded contours is in proportion to the strength of sunlight in any given country. In sunless England, for example, mouldings were more coarse, while in sun-filled Greece they were more refined.*

IAN C. STEWART

IAN C. STEWART

IAN C. STEWART

IAN C. STEWART

IAN C. STEWART

LEFT: The north side of Koon Seng Road. The 13 houses set back from the road with their own forecourts are a stylish example of Straits Chinese architecture.

R. IAN LLOYD

BELOW: *Nos. 2-16 along the south side of Koon Seng Road, a portrait of stylish, spruce painted ladies — from the red roof tiles, to the carved timber fascia boards; from the heavily decorated entablature above the second storey windows, to the bas-relief below depicting animals associated with good luck by the Chinese; from the Ionic-style pilasters to the decorative corbels; from the petal-shaped air vents above the first storey windows to the pintu pagar.*

THIAN HOCK KENG

Singapore's oldest Chinese temple is also the most authentic example of traditional Chinese temple architecture extant today.

The temple's location is no accident. In 1824, five years after Singapore's founding, a census revealed that there were more than 3,300 Chinese settlers on the island. Many immigrants had sailed across perilous seas. On arrival, they set up shrines to the various deities as a gesture of thanks – such as the joss house erected by Hokkien settlers just above the then shoreline of Telok Ayer Street in 1819.

Between 1839-1842 a large, grand, syncretic temple, the Temple of the Goddess of Heaven, was constructed on the same site. Funds came from wealthy merchants, like Tan Kim Seng and Tan Tock Seng, who wanted to show their spirit of leadership and to thank the Gods for their good fortune.

Skilled crafstmen and all of the building materials were especially imported from China for the project. These anonymous designers and craftsmen followed definite Chinese temple architectural traditions.

The skill of the craftsmen can be seen in features like the intricate and ornate columns, sculpted from solid blocks of granite and the elaborate and complicated carved painted roof forms, the main structural element of the temple's beam and bracket system which supports the roof and the overhanging eaves and is both aesthetic and practical.

A number of restorations have been carried out over the years. As early as 1888 the pagoda was renovated and in 1906 a new front gate was added. Between 1976-79 a major effort was undertaken by the Hokkien Hui Guan, the present owners of the temple. Skilled craftsmen were called upon once again and the essential repairs were sensitively executed to restore the temple to the state it was in over a century ago when wealthy Hokkien merchants congregated to celebrate its opening.

R IAN LLOYD

RIGHT: The main courtyard. The temple, modelled on a courtyard house plan, is in the best tradition of 19th century Southern Chinese architecture. The main diety, Tian Hou, Goddess of Seafarers, is worshipped in the central hall.

R. IAN LLOYD

LEFT: One of the dragons gracing the main roof ridge of the temple.

BELOW: A roof which appears to be almost "floating" without walls. The steep overhang of the front eaves casts a shadow on the temple's front entrance dimming but not hiding the richness of the front entrance.

R. IAN LLOYD

R. IAN LLOYD

R. IAN LLOYD

R. IAN LLOYD

R. IAN LLOYD

Four interior views.
LEFT ABOVE: The elaborately carved roof brackets, part of the support system of the temple roof.
RIGHT ABOVE: Painted laquer, carved granite and carved timber panels give added richness and drama to the ceiling.
BELOW LEFT: One of the temple's intricately carved granite pillars.
BELOW RIGHT: More of the richly carved beam and bracket supports.

SULTAN MOSQUE

IAN C. STEWART

The Mosque, framed by the buildings of Bussorah Street.

In 1823, provision was made for Sultan Hussein to build a "respectable mosque" near his new Istana in Kampong Glam and Raffles even promised $3,000 towards the cost. Raffles had moved the Sultan and his followers to a 24.6 ha village east of the European town, an area lying between Rochore river and the sea, bounded by Middle Road, Jalan Sultan, Beach Road and North Bridge Road. He had also indicated that it was near the new Istana that Arabs, Bugis and other followers of the Islamic faith were to settle.

The original Masjid Sultan, or Sultan Mosque, was a simple structure with a three-tier tiled roof. It was probably completed circa 1824. When North Bridge Road was constructed in 1825 it was diverted slightly to the north to avoid the mosque. The mosque is not Singapore's oldest; that distinction belongs to Masjid Omar Kampong Melaka built in Kampong Malacca in 1820 by the Arab trader Syed Omar bin Ali Al-Junied and extensively renovated in 1982.

The 1824 building served admirably for a century. Then, in 1924, the versatile firm of Swan and Maclaren was appointed to build a new mosque. Under the direction of Denis Santry the present gilt onion shaped dome building was erected. The mosque is the only example of Saracenic architecture (also known as Islamic or Muslim architecture and a mixture of Persian, Turkish, Moorish and Indian elements) extant in Singapore, although several other buildings in this style were constructed around the same time.

Gazetted as a national monument in 1975, the mosque subsequently underwent extensive repairs and remodelling. As with other mosques in Singapore it is administered by the Muslim Religious Council and managed by a group of Trustees. There are over 100 mosques and *surau* in Singapore today, but Sultan Mosque remains a focal point for many Muslims on the island.

R. IAN LLOYD

R. IAN LLOYD

LEFT: *Roof details. One of the four corner minarets, the small decorative turrets and cresting set along the roof parapet.*

ABOVE: *One of the two onion-shaped gilt domes. A unique feature of the Mosque is the use of green bottles embedded into the base of the domes.*

IAN C. STEWART

IAN C. STEWART

IAN C. STEWART

IAN C. STEWART

Four details frequently seen in Saracenic architecture.
TOP LEFT: *A pair of Saracenic arches.*
TOP RIGHT: *A trio of pointed trefoil arches enclose a balcony.*
BOTTOM LEFT: *A trio of cinquefoil windows.*
BOTTOM RIGHT: *Detail of the cast iron fence surrounding the Mosque grounds.*

SRI MARIAMMAN TEMPLE

The Sri Mariamman Temple on South Bridge Road is the oldest Hindu place of worship still in use.

The man responsible for its birth was Naraina Pillai, a Penang merchant and the first recorded Indian immigrant to Singapore. He accompanied Raffles on the ship Indiana on Raffles' second visit here in May 1819. Pillai was an enterprising, versatile man. He started his own brick kiln and became Singapore's first contractor. He was also a clerk in the government and had his own textile shop. When a fire burned the textile shop in 1822 and wiped him out, it was Raffles who helped him rebuild his fortune.

As a leader of the Hindu community, Pillai wished to establish a place of Hindu worship. The authorities first granted him a strip of land in Telok Ayer Street, but, since there was no fresh water nearby, he was allowed to exchange it for another site near Stamford Road Canal, then known as Freshwater Stream. The Town Planning Committee of 1822-23 did not agree to this – there were other plans for that part of town – and he moved in early 1823 to the present South Bridge Road site.

By 1827, a wood and attap temple had been constructed and circa 1840 it was replaced by a more permanent brick building. The present building is believed to date from 1862-63, and was built by Indian and Chinese craftsmen following the general ground plan which has not altered since 1844.

The decorations on the building have been redone many times. The gopuram, or tower, at the gateway was fully established by 1903 and it was given a major facelift in 1923. In 1910 the attap-covered way between the gateway and the main building was destroyed by fire and in 1915-16 Swan and Maclaren designed a new covered way.

The temple is owned and administered by the Hindu Endowments Board. It was gazetted as a national monument in 1973.

IAN C. STEWART

The tall, massive, studded timber doors protect a courtyard and central hall. Singapore's Hindu temples generally follow closely the designs and forms of the temples of Southern India and, in the early days, they were largely designed and built by anonymous skilled craftsmen.

KOUO SHANG-WEI

RIGHT: A Hindu temple consists of three basic elements: A shrine for the Gods, a hall for worshippers and a gopuram. The 15 m high gopuram of Sri Mariamman has been a landmark on South Bridge Road since the temple's founding in 1827. The present version dates from 1923. The colourful, sculptures represent the divine trinity of Veda mythology – Brahma, Vishnu and Shiva.

OVERLEAF: The covered walkway to the hall of the temple looking towards the shrine. It was constructed in the early 20th century. The ceiling is colourfully painted with characters from Hindu mythology.

IAN C. STEWART

THE ARMENIAN CHURCH

"The small, but elegant building does great credit to the public spirit and religious feeling of the Armenians of this settlement; for we believe that few instances could be shown where so small a community have contributed funds sufficient for the erection of a similar edifice.
The design was by Mr. G.D. Coleman and whether owing to the abilities of the workmen, or the vigilance with which that gentleman superintended them we know not, but it appears to us that the Armenian Church is one of the most ornate and best finished pieces of architecture that this gentleman can boast of."

– Singapore Free Press (1836).

The Armenian Church has the distinction of being the oldest church in Singapore. Dedicated to St Gregory the Illuminator, the first monk of the Armenian Church, it was built in the open fields at the foot of Fort Canning on government land in 1835.

There was a small, prosperous Armenian community here, including three Armenian business firms, as early as 1821 when the first religious service was celebrated. The church's old minute book shows that on 8 January 1825 a meeting was held to prepare a letter to one of the Archbishops in Persia asking for a priest to be sent to Singapore. More correspondence followed and, in 1827, a meeting was held to collect money and to decide on a permanent place to hold services.

It was natural that such a prosperous community would choose the best architect available. G.D. Coleman, the talented Irish architect who had already established an undisputed reputation in the settlement, was the man appointed to build the new church.

Coleman was born in Drogheda County in Ireland in 1795. History has not recorded where he was educated. His name appears neither on the registers of the Dublin Society nor of the Royal Academy School in London, but he must have received a good classical training, given his familiarity with the Palladian and Georgian architecture then prevalent in Great Britain.

In 1815, Coleman left Europe for Calcutta where he practised as an architect, building mostly private houses for merchants. In 1820, he made his way further east to Batavia, in Java, where he practiced architecture and surveying. Coleman was in Singapore in 1822, early records show, and Raffles sought his advice on the Town Plan. Coleman, no doubt, saw ample opportunities for work in the young settlement and moved to Singapore in 1826 to take up the post of Revenue Surveyor.

Small yet elegant, the Armenian church is one of the three Coleman buildings still standing and is undoubtedly his masterpiece. The church is not only a skilful marriage of the Palladian style with the demands of the tropical climate, but a beautiful example of his inventiveness and ingenuity.

The main structure of the church is a circle, 36 feet in diameter, superimposed on a square plan with projecting square porticoes on all four sides. Each portico is surmounted by simple pediments supported by six columns built with Roman Doric orders. The wide verandahs provide ample shade and louvred windows reduce glare, provide protection against heavy rain and encourage the highly desirable cross ventilation.

The Armenian Church set a high aesthetic standard for religious buildings throughout the 19th century. It was completed in January, 1835 at a cost of $5,058.30, with $400 received by Coleman as architect's fees. The building has remained basically unaltered since Coleman's time, except for the replacement around 1850 of the original octagonal cone roof and bell turret with the present pitched roof, tower and spire. It was gazetted as a national monument in 1973.

IAN C. STEWART

LEFT: The interior of the church is simple, with rudimentary mouldings. Note the original timber louvred windows.

RIGHT: Coleman employed the standard Palladian themes of pedimented porticoes, single or couple Doric columns and pilasters on a symmetrical plan. The plan of the building appeared to have its origin in that of a church dedicated to St Gregory in Echmiadzin, near Erivan, in north Armenia, although it was also inspired by James Gibb's first circular design for St Martin in the Fields, London, published in his Book of Architecture, London, 1728.

KOUO SHANG-WEI

THONG CHAI MEDICAL INSTITUTION

Completed in 1892, the Thong Chai Medical Institution building in Wayang Street is one of the only non-religious buildings remaining in Singapore which was constructed in pure Chinese style. Around the same time as Thong Chai was built, four wealthy Chinese merchants constructed homes in a similar pure Chinese style, but only one remains: the house built by wealthy Teochew gambier and pepper merchant Tan Yeok Nee in 1885 on Clemenceau Avenue which is now the Salvation Army headquarters.

R. IAN LLOYD

The Thong Chai building is a two-storey structure in southern Chinese palace style with two inner courts. The internal decorative carvings on the roof supports and beams, doors and windows are in the best tradition of Chinese craftsmen who were active in the building industry in Singapore from the late 19th century onwards, especially in the fields of carpentry, joinery, carving and decorative plasterwork.

R. IAN LLOYD

The Institution was originally established in 1867 as a free hospital. Funds for the Wayang Street building were amassed with the aid of public subscriptions and donations. Mr Gan Eng Seng, a noted philanthropist of the day, was the chief benefactor.

The building was acquired by the Government and gazetted as a national monument to "manifest the spirit of mutual assistance among the early Chinese settlers" in 1973. It is now owned by the Preservation of Monuments Board and leased out. It continues a useful purpose as an arts and crafts centre.

R. IAN LLOYD

LEFT AND ABOVE: Thong Chai has a roof-scape like no other in Singapore — a series of roofs embellished with cloud-shaped gable ends, pronounced roof ridges with flamboyant decorations and glazed green tiles.

R. IAN LLOYD

RIGHT: Interior view. The timber frieze of Chinese geometric pattern lends further definition to the division between the courtyard and the interior spaces. The calligraphy is actually the second half of a pair of panels, or couplet, and reads "Administer charity to all things with the heart of a saint and a sage".

The appeal of this ceiling lies in the use of construction details for aesthetic effect. Here the clear expression of the roof supports is a pleasing counterpoint to the calligraphy.

ST JOSEPH'S INSTITUTION

"In the beginning of 1865 the Brother Director, Brother Lothaire, determined to set to work to provide a new schoolhouse, to be used as a school and a dwelling house for the Brothers. In February, 1865 he wrote to the Government that he had been promised $4,500 for the purpose, and sent a plan of the proposed building. He asked Government for assistance, but the only result was the grant of Government bricks at the cost price to Government, and even this was not fully carried out, as the building of the new Government House required so many bricks that the promise to the School was set aside before the building was finished. On 8th November 1866, Brother Lothaire made a contract with a Chinese for the construction of the building . . ."

– *As quoted in An Anecdotal History of Old Times in Singapore 1819-1865 by C.B. Buckley.*

St Joseph's Institution is an outstanding example of the architectural contribution made by a group of French Catholic priest-architects in the 19th and early 20th centuries. The domed central block was designed by Brother Lothaire, one of the six Brothers brought out by Father Beurel in 1852 to establish a boys' school. Beurel himself had arrived in Singapore in 1837 and spent nearly 30 years here, working tirelessly to fulfil his dream of providing an education to boys and girls regardless of race or religion. Father Beurel's dream was realised with the opening of both St Joseph's Institution and the Convent of the Holy Infant Jesus.

The boy's school, financed by private subscriptions and Beurel's own personal fortune, opened its doors in 1852 in a wood and attap house. In 1855, the foundation stone of a new building was laid, but lack of funds delayed the project for nearly a decade. Finally, in 1865, plans for the proposed new school were submitted to the government and, two years later, it was completed. The government had promised to sell bricks to the Brothers at cost price but the building of the Government House (Istana) required so many bricks that the promise was never fulfilled.

The school is on the site of Singapore's first Catholic church, built in 1830. The church closed after the opening of the Cathedral of the Good Shepherd across the street, which was completed in 1846 to the design of Denis Leslie McSwiney, another early architect.

Brother Lothaire and his contemporaries were well-equipped for the task of designing ecclesiastical buildings. Urbane and well-educated, they were well-acquainted with the Classical traditions and would have studied the principles of architecture as part of their training.

The gracious curved wings of the building, circa 1900, were designed by another priest-architect, Father Nain, who was also responsible for the design of the chapel in the Convent of the Holy Infant Jesus. The gymnasium and chapel behind the main building of St Joseph's were added in 1911-12.

IAN C. STEWART

IAN C. STEWART

FAR LEFT: The graceful form of the crescent-shaped wings abutting the main block is clearly evident.
LEFT: The front portico offers a generous, shady space.

IAN C. STEWART

LEFT: A frontal view. St Joseph's is a Classical hybrid. Classical elements, in this case with a French reference, were simplified and modified by the architect-priest-builders of the 19th century who were responsible for designing many such schools and churches around the world. The front portico, with its semi-circular pediment, together with the dome-shaped clerestory create a strong focal point and accentuate the symmetry of the building form.

RIGHT: Within the well-proportioned verandah students do their last minute studying. The unbroken colonnade provides sheltered space for pedestrian movement and creates an interesting interplay of light and shade.

IAN C. STEWART

RAFFLES HOTEL

It was a partnership destined for success. Three Armenian brothers named Sarkies, shrewd entrepreneurs with experience in the hotel business, hired the leading architectural firm of the day, Swan and Maclaren, to prepare a massive renovation plan for their hotel. Regent Alfred John Bidwell, who had graduated from the Architectural Association in London with honours in design and who was fresh from designing the Saracenic Government Secretariat in Kuala Lumpur, was assigned the task. The result: a splendidly elegant hotel.

The Sarkies brothers arrived in Singapore in the mid-1880s with the intention of expanding their hotel empire. Although the hotel business centred around the Esplanade, High Street and Coleman Street, they bought a bungalow at the corner of the Beach Road and Bras Basah Road from Captain and Mrs Dare who operated an established Tiffin Room with a good reputation. The year: 1886.

It was a modest start. Beach Road, the most salubrious residential area in the earlier part of the century, was, by now, seedy and run-down. But the shoreline was at the edge of the aptly-named Beach Road and the site offered an unparalleled view of the harbour and the seas beyond.

The Sarkies carried out a series of additions and renovations, gradually upgrading their establishment. The most ambitious scheme started in 1897 under Bidwell's direction. Not only were the Sarkies anticipating the redevelopment of the Beach Road area, they were also conscious of the fact that their main competitor, the Hotel d'Europe, which stood at the corner now occupied by the Supreme Court, was also undertaking large-scale renovations (also by Swan and Maclaren). But the most significant factor was the rapid growth of the port. By the turn of the century Singapore was the seventh busiest port in the world.

The new wing opened on 18 November 1899 and was soon known as "the Savoy of the Orient". For Swan and Maclaren, the commission marked the first of a series which, thanks to Bidwell's able talent, firmly established the firm's pre-eminence only 12 years after its founding in 1887.

". . . a building of noble proportions and imposing appearance and covers an area of no less than 200,000 square feet. It commands an unrivalled panoramic view of the harbour and the adjacent islands and is conveniently situated within easy reach of the chief business centres. On the ground floor is the marble-paved dining room, than which there is probably none more handsome in the East; whilst the spacious open verandah is one of the breeziest spots in Singapore. The private dining rooms form an important feature and are in constant demand . . ."

– *Twentieth Century Impressions of British Malaya (1908).*

RIGHT: The Raffles Hotel, circa 1900s. The 1890s renovation entailed the demolition of an existing block and the erection in its place of a new three-storey building consisting of a facade with a pedimented central section facing Beach Road with short splayed wings at each end. The building had its own generator to supply lights, lift and fans — major innovations at the time.

BELOW: The Palm Court. The tropical garden space is as important to the historic hotel as are the buildings which surround it.

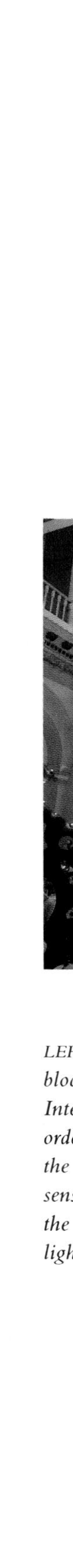

R. IAN LLOYD

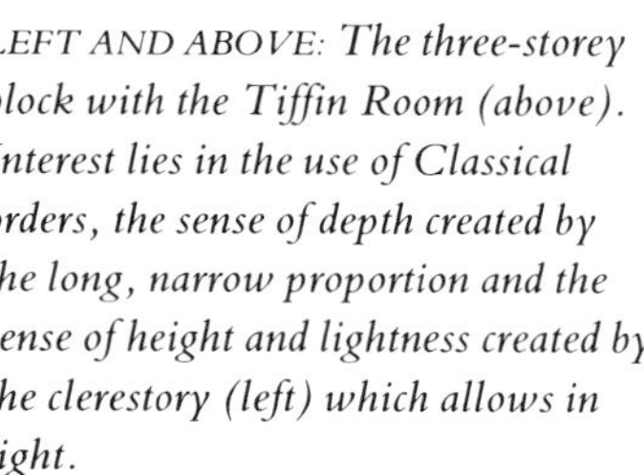

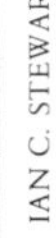

IAN C. STEWART

LEFT AND ABOVE: *The three-storey block with the Tiffin Room (above). Interest lies in the use of Classical orders, the sense of depth created by the long, narrow proportion and the sense of height and lightness created by the clerestory (left) which allows in light.*

PUBLIC BUILDINGS

". . . and Colonel Farquhar finding that Sir Stamford was giving away land very fast, protested, and desired Raffles to make a reference to Bengal on his proposition to retain eight hundred yards on the north beach. Sir Stamford did not forward the reference, but reserved the ground from the Singapore River to the Bras Basah Canal, and it should be added, that we are indebted, therefore, to Colonel Farquhar for the present Esplanade."

– Referring to the year 1822, C.B. Buckley in An Anecdotal History of Old Times in Singapore, 1819-1865 by C.B. Buckley.

Singapore's colonial Palladian, Gothic, Victorian, Neo-Renaissance and Neo-Classical public buildings span a period of less than one hundred years, from the opening of the Town Hall, now Victoria Theatre, in 1855, to the Supreme Court Building completed in 1939. The one exception is Parliament House. It was built as the private residence of merchant J.A. Maxwell by G.D. Coleman in 1827 and was bought over by the government in 1841.

During the last half of the 19th century, the pace of construction of public buildings was stepped up to accommodate the needs of the rapidly expanding town. The development coincided with two significant events: The opening of the Suez Canal in 1869, which led to more trade and increased prosperity for the settlement, and the transfer of rule from India to the Colonial Office in London which meant, among other things, more efficient management of the city.

Nearly all of the early public buildings were designed by engineers from the Madras Artillery who joined the Public Works Department or its earlier equivalent. The two most famous personalities were Lieut. Col. Ronald MacPherson who arrived in 1852 and was Executive Engineer and Superintendent of Convicts. He designed St Andrew's Cathedral and became the first Colonial Secretary of the Crown Colony of Singapore in 1867. His successor, Major J.F.A. McNair, came in 1856. McNair retained the post for 16 years and finally became Resident Councillor in Penang.

Many of the early important public buildings centre around Empress Place and the Padang, which was known as the Plain or Esplanade. It was Raffles who dictated that the government buildings should be located there on the north side of the Singapore River. Today the area remains a focal point of the city. The buildings have admirably survived the political transition and lend a sense of dignity, constancy and history to the fast-changing city.

KOUO SHANG-WEI

LEFT:
Victoria Theatre and Memorial Hall, Empress Place.

The Theatre (left) was built as a Town Hall in 1856–62 and provided space for government offices and a stage for theatrical entertainment. When the community decided to build a new theatre to commemorate the Jubilee celebrations of Queen Victoria at the turn of the century, Swan and Maclaren were appointed. Their design solution: To integrate a new hall with the re-faced existing theatre and join the two with a 60 m clock tower. Ground was broken in 1902. Upon completion in 1906, the complex became a civic landmark and so it is today. The building is a hybrid of Classical and Renaissance elements with an interesting interplay of textures and patterns — all adapted to suit the tropical climate. The clock tower not only strengthens the symmetry of the building but acts as an important focal point in the city.

BELOW:
The Supreme Court and City Hall, St. Andrew's Road.

The Supreme Court (foreground) was built in 1937–39 and marked the final use of Classical Orders for a public building here. The two sets of Ionic columns on either side of the front porch highlight the austerity of the building while the large dome and elaborate pediment reinforce its symmetry. Designed by F. Dorrington-Ward and built by United Engineers, the building's sculpture, columns and facing were executed by Cav. R. Nolli. Nolli was one of a party of Italian artists who came East in 1913 at the invitation of the King of Siam to build a new throne room in Bangkok. He arrived in Singapore in 1921 and may well have been responsible for the "Italianate" or "Renaissance" plasterwork on so many of the smaller buildings of this period. City Hall (background) was built in 1926–29 to the design of F.D. Meadows. The two make an imposing presence, especially when seen from across the open green space of the Padang.

KOUO SHANG-WEI

IAN C. STEWART

Former Hill Street Police Station, Hill Street and River Valley Road.

Completed in 1936, this imposing presence is 100 m long and six storeys high. The cantilevered sixth storey and projecting bays of the fifth storey add further interest to the facade as does the long splayed corner. The building is an interesting, rather late interpretation of Classical-inspired Public Works architecture.

KOUO SHANG-WEI

KOUO SHANG-WEI

Singapore Fire Brigade HQ Building, Hill Street.

LEFT: The fire brigade was established in 1888, but it wasn't until 1909 that the main block of this brick "Blood and Bandage" building was erected. The "Blood", or exposed brick, and "Bandage", brick which has been covered in plaster and painted white, was a popular style in Edwardian England circa the early 20th century. In Singapore, its use marked a significant departure from the Palladian and other Classical themes so popular in Government buildings.

BELOW: Ionic-style columns and elegant plasterwork and two of the "Blood and Bandage" arched doorways.

IAN C. STEWART

IAN C. STEWART

IAN C. STEWART

Istana
Designed by J.F.A. McNair and built between 1867 and 1869 by Indian convict labourers who made their own bricks, cement and plaster, the Istana is today the official residence of the President of Singapore. From 1869 until 1959, this well-proportioned building with simple Ionic and Doric type columns was known as Government House and was the official residence of the British Governor. This postcard, circa 1900s, gives a grand sense of the building's domain which was, originally, part of a nutmeg plantation owned by C.R. Prinsep.

HOUSES

Large bungalows and villas built before World War II are a dying species. Many have been demolished in the wake of rapid urbanisation. Nonetheless, these houses – and some fine examples still exist – constitute an important element of Singapore's architectural heritage and merit a brief description.

A turn-of-the-century bungalow on sturdy brick piers with a verandah along three sides.
The drawing is from the collection of building plans dating back to 1887 housed in the National Archives.

The first houses here were hastily erected timber and attap buildings constructed for the early merchants. As Singapore's future became more secure and trade flourished these men built impressive homes in the town area, along High Street and Coleman Street as well as in the Beach Road area. G.D. Coleman himself designed several homes with a Palladian theme between 1828 and 1844 which set a high standard for other builders. Climate, of course, was a major consideration and house plans had to be open to allow for the maximum ventilation of air.

Outside the town area, the first permanent houses were probably built for plantation owners. They eschewed the fancy Palladian treatment and were simple, functional buildings based on the Malay house and built in timber or brick on sturdy brick piers with verandahs extending around three or all four sides for maximum weather protection.

The houses of the later part of the 19th and early 20th century retained the theme of the Malay house but saw the infusion of Chinese and European elements. It is difficult to imagine a city of such homes today but the building plans housed in National Archives' records centre give some indication of the variety and richness of detail of these homes, from the more humble single-storey kampong house with Malay fretwork eaves built on low brick piers with a front verandah, to the elaborate two-storey villas with Venetian windows, Corinthian style columns columns and ornate plasterwork.

The period between 1920 and 1940 was one of transition as the airy, high-ceiling villas and bungalows evolved into low-ceiling, smaller-roomed modern houses. The advent of modern architecture, the general use of modern sanitation, re-inforced concrete and electricity were all factors which contributed to a different expression of house design.

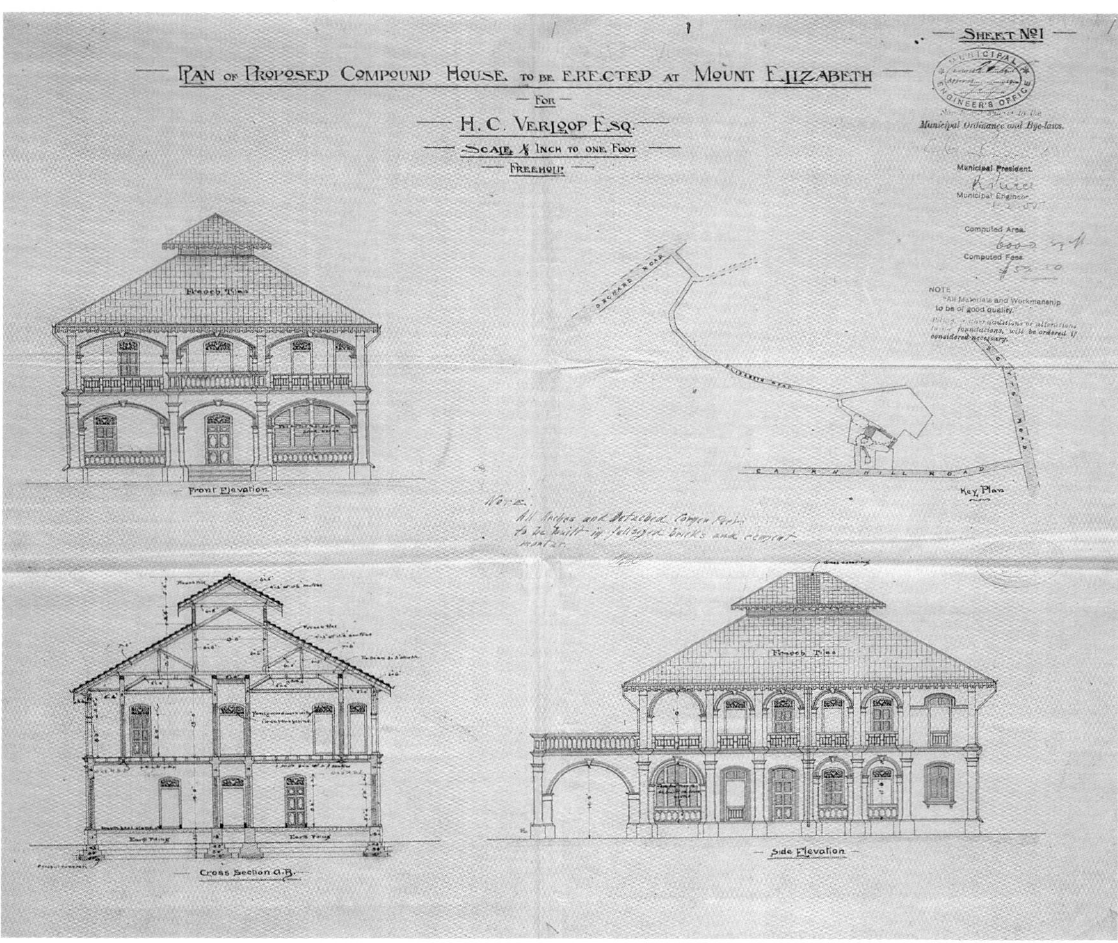

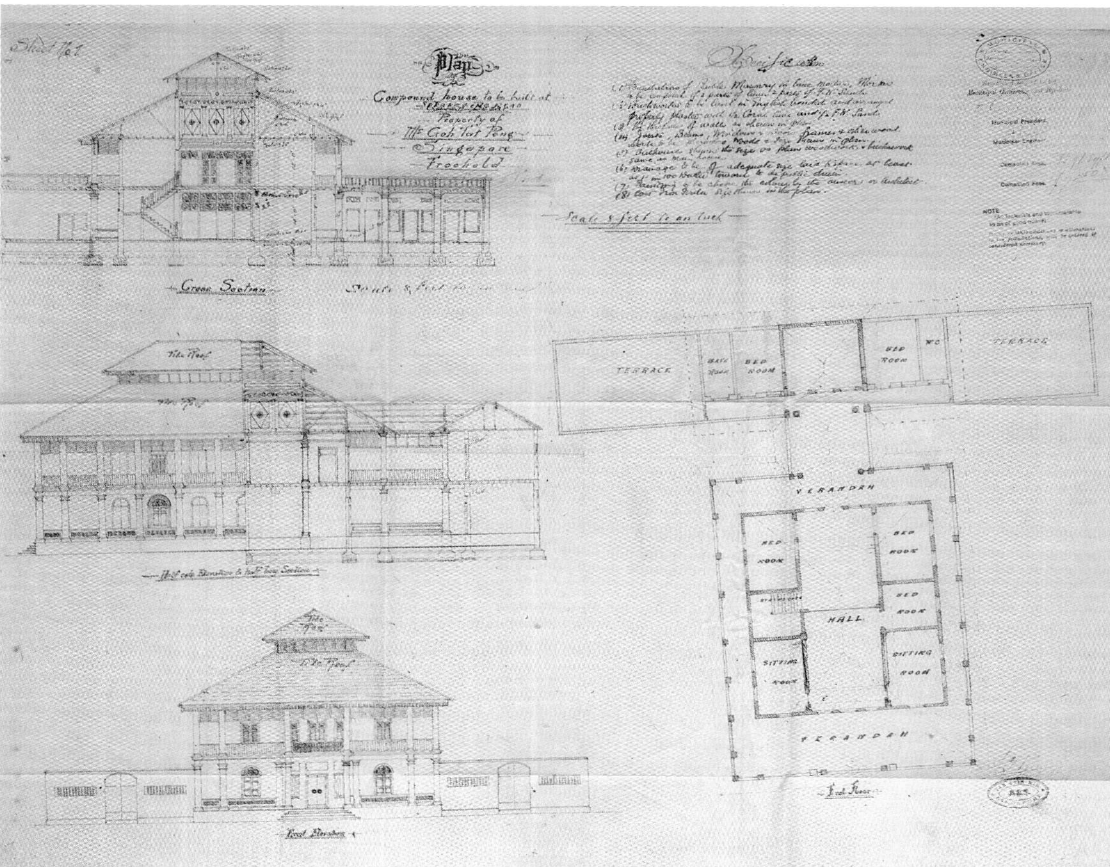

R. IAN LLOYD

R. IAN LLOYD

LEFT: More turn-of-the century plans, but for more ornate two-storey villas. Note the sketch map on the plan for Mr. H. C. Verloop at Mount Elizabeth (above). Nearly all of the early plans have these roughly drawn maps which give countless clues to the growth and development of the city. The house for Mr Goh Tat Peng (below) has a symmetrical floor plan. Note the separation of the servant's quarters from the main building. Both houses have jack roofs for better ventilation and cooling protective verandahs encircling both the first and second storeys. The carved timber panels, shutters and fascia boards are also drawn in.

A "freestanding" villa (far left) in an urban area modified to fit its environment at No. 37 Kerbau Road. What would have been a front portico is a five-foot way created by the overhang of the first storey. The pintu pagar (far left, below) is heavily carved.

LEFT: The front entrance of No. 37 Kerbau Road is a classic example of Straits Chinese architecture. Note the timber lintels which support the upper storey and the pair of scrolls above the windows. The calligraphy panel above the door, an important element of these houses, represents the marriage of art — the calligraphy — and craftsmanship — the carving. The characters mean "Elegant or Refined Pine", the pine being a symbol of endurance, and express the owner's hopes, aspirations or inspiration for the character of those who live in the house.

BELOW: Traditionally the most important room, the front hall is dominated by a shrine to the gods and the tablets for ancestors. Interesting architectural features include Malacca tiles of unglazed fired clay, a pair of scrolls painted onto the wall and a lavish carved swinging gate between the front hall and the room behind. The Straits Chinese taste in furniture was an eclectic mixture of Chinese, European (Victorian) and a blending of the two executed in local woods, frequently teak. Here we see the original altar tables and the rosewood or blackwood Mother-of-Pearl inlaid chairs.

IAN C. STEWART

A Selection of Black and White Houses. An adaptive, eclectic cross between a Malay kampong house and the buildings of Tudor England (1485–1558), Singapore's black and white houses were mostly built during the heady days of the post-War rubber boom during the 1920s. They provided quarters for senior British civil servants and were designed by municipal or government architects and engineers who, by then, knew well how to beat the rigours of the tropical climate. While the black painted half–timbering and white plasterwork provided a nostalgic reminder of home, the very functional wood and attap kampong house provided the basic inspiration. Many of the houses have no windows at all and overhangs, balconies, verandahs and chick blinds provided weather protection. There are many good examples of one-and two-storey black and white houses in Goodwood Hill, Adam Park, Malcolm Road, Cluny and Dalvey Roads, Mount Pleasant, Ridley Park and Seaton Close/ Nassim Road. They are owned by the government and rented out.

IAN C. STEWART

IAN C. STEWART

IAN C STEWART

No. 358 River Valley Road, built for Khoo Yang Tin Esq. in 1936 by Chung Hong Woot and Wong. A two-storey building of reinforced concrete resting on sturdy columns, the house is typical of those built by wealthy Chinese families. In front of the house is a semi-circular garden with numerous trees, a fountain and a pavilion surrounded by a sturdy wall. The house is symmetrical on a cross-shaped plan with detached servants quarters. Note the Classical details, the plasterwork, the carved timber fretwork fascia boards, the large windows and the pitched roof with wide overhangs to protect against rain and sun.

BIBLIOGRAPHY

BOOKS AND EXHIBITION CATALOGUES

Archives and Oral History Department; *Chinatown, An Album of a Singapore Community*; Times Books International, (Singapore, 1983).

Archives and Oral History Department; *Singapore Retrospective Through Postcards 1900-1930*; Sin Chew Jit Poh, (Singapore, 1982).

Berry, Linda; *Singapore's River, A Living Legacy*; Eastern Universities Press, (Singapore, 1982).

Buckley, C.B.; *An Anecdotal History of Old Times in Singapore. 1819-1867*; The University of Malaya Press, (Kuala Lumpur, 1965).

Cameron, John; *Our Tropical Possessions in Malayan India*; First published in London in 1865, reprinted by Oxford University Press, (Kuala Lumpur, 1965).

Doggett, Marjorie; *Characters of Light*; Donald Moore Press, (Singapore, 1957).

Fletcher, Banister; *A History of Architecture on the Comparative Method*; B.T. Batsford Press, (London, 1956).

Gan Eng Oon, Editor; *RUMAH, Contemporary Architecture in Singapore*; Singapore Institute of Architects, (Singapore, 1981).

Hancock, T.H.H. and Gibson-Hill, C.A.; *Architecture in Singapore*, Exhibition Catalogue; (Singapore, 1954).

Hooi, Christopher; *National Monuments of Singapore;* The National Museum (Singapore, 1982).

Journal of the Malaysian Branch of the Royal Asiatic Society; Singapore, 150 Years; Times Books International, (Singapore, 1982).

Jones, John Hall and Hooi, Christopher; *An Early Surveyor in Singapore*; National Museum, (Singapore, 1979).

Jones Lang Wootton; *Our Heritage is Worth Preserving*, Exhibition Catalogue; (Singapore, 1983).

Lip, Evelyn; *Chinese Temple Architecture in Singapore*; Singapore University Press, (Singapore, 1983).

Ministry of Culture; *The Singapore Heritage*; (Singapore, 1983).

National Museum of Singapore; *Singapore Rediscovered*, Exhibition Catalogue; (Singapore, 1983).

Sharp, Ilsa; *There is Only One Raffles*; Souvenir Press for Times Publishing, (Singapore, 1982).

Siddique, Sharon and Shotam, Nirmala Puru; *Singapore's Little India, Past Present and Future*; Institute of Southeast Asian Studies, (Singapore, 1982).

Song Ong Siang; *One Hundred Years of the Chinese in Singapore*, University of Malaya Press, (Singapore, 1967).

Turnbull, C.M.; *A History of Singapore, 1819-1975*; Oxford University Press, (Kuala Lumpur, 1977).

Tyers, Ray; *Singapore Then and Now*, Two Volumes; University Education Press, (Singapore, 1976).

UNPUBLISHED THESES AND ACADEMIC EXERCISES

Seow, Eu Jin; *Architectural Development in Singapore*; PhD Thesis, (University of Melbourne, 1974).

Ang, Lian Neo; *The Straits Chinese House: its architecture and artifacts*, (National University of Singapore, 1980-81).

Boey, Yut Mei; *Kampong Glam: a Community;* (NUS, 1973-74).

Chan, Ken Meng; *Conservation of Chinatown;* (NUS, 1975-76).

Foong, Chai Yoong; *Chinatown House;* (NUS, 1970-71).

Tan, How Koh; *The Ann Siang Hill Study: A Review*; (NUS, 1981-82).

Tan, Quee Huat; *The Character of the Singapore Riverside*; (NUS, 1972-73).

Tan, Siok Lay; *Image of Tanjong Pagar as a Physical Environment*; (NUS, 1972-73).

Teo, Hong Kee; *A Study of Pagoda Street*; (NUS, 1975-76).

Woo, Pei Li; *Swan & Maclaren: Singapore's pioneer firm in architecture*; (NUS, 1980-81).

MAGAZINE ARTICLES

Keys, Peter; "Straits Chinese Terrace Houses in Singapore"; *Orientations Magazine* (June 1983), pp. 43-53.

Mahbubani, Gretchen; "Pioneering Plans"; *The Straits Times Annual* (1982), pp. 80-101.

Lee, Kip Lin and Yeh, Ding Shin; "The Beauty of Chinese Baroque"; *The Straits Times Annual* (1977), pp. 23-28.

GLOSSARY

arcade A series of arches supported on piers or columns.

architrave The moulded frame around a door or window.

Art Deco A decorative style of design stimulated by the Paris Exposition International des Arts Decoratifs et Undustrielles Moderne which was held in Paris in 1925 and widely used in the architecture of the 1930s.

atap, attap A Malay word for roofing or thatch; made with the leaves of a palm tree.

bas-relief A carving, embossing or casting which protrudes slightly from its background plane.

bungalow A one-storey house, lightly built, usually with a tiled or thatched roof and encircling verandah; the word is derived from the Hindi word 'bangla' meaning belonging to Bengal. In Singapore, the term is used to describe almost any detached house irrespective of its height or form.

cantilever Any part of a structure which projects beyond its supporting element.

capital The top member of a column or pilaster.

casement A window or ventilator which opens outwards for its full height.

chunam From the Tamil word for lime, chunnam; a cement or plaster made of shell lime and sea sand, originating in India.

Classic The term used to describe the art of Hellenic Greece and Imperial Rome on which the Italian Renaissance based its development. The five Orders of architecture are a characteristic feature.

cloisters Covered passageways around a space.

colonnade A row of columns.

column A vertical support usually consisting of a base, a circular shaft and a capital.

Composite Order An order of architecture used by the Romans, with a capital composed of both Corinthian and Ionic features.

corbel From the French word for a raven, hence a beak-like projection; a block of masonry projecting from a wall supporting a roof, floor, vault or other architectural feature and often elaborately carved.

Corinthian Order The third order of Greek architecture.

cornice A crowning projection, but more usually referring to the uppermost portion of the entablature in Classic or Renaissance architecture.

dentils Tooth-like cubes used in Ionic and Corinthian cornices.

Doric Order The first and simplest order of Greek architecture which was also used by the Romans in a simplified form and with a base.

eaves The lower part of a roof which projects beyond the supporting structure.

eclectic In architectural terms, a style which is derived from the borrowing of a selection of elements from other styles.

Edwardian architecture Architecture of the reign of King Edward VII of England (1901–1910).

elevation Literally, a drawing of a building made in projection on a vertical plane but now more commonly used to describe the vertical face of a building itself.

entablature The upper part of an Order of architecture which consists of an architrave, frieze and cornice, supported by a colonnade.

facade The face or elevation of a building.

fascia A vertical face of small projections. In the Ionic and Corinthian Orders the architraves are divided into two or more such bands.

finial An ornament placed upon the apex of a roof, spire, pediment or at each corner of a tower.

fluting Vertical channelling, usually applied to a column or pilaster.

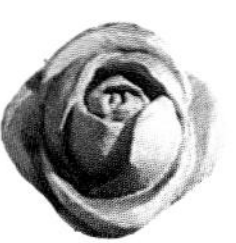

fret	In Classical or Renaissance architecture this term referred to an ornament consisting of straight lines intersecting at right angles and of various patterns but now it also refers to timber work which has been decorated by cutting patterns with a fret saw.
frieze	The middle division of the Classic entablature between the cornice above and the architrave below; also, a similar decorative band near the top of an interior wall below the cornice.
godown	An Asian expression for a warehouse or goods store derived from the Anglo-Indian.
Gopuram	A Southern Indian word for the monumental gateway of a temple.
Gothic Revival	A movement which originated in the late 18th century with the intention of reviving the forms, if not the spirit, of Gothic architecture.
Gothic style	The style of pointed Mediaeval architecture which developed in Western Europe between the 13th and 15th centuries and was succeeded by the Classic forms of the Renaissance.
High Renaissance	The peak of the Renaissance period.
hu lu	A bottle shaped symbol meant to protect against evil spirits.
Ionic Order	The second Order of Ionian Greek architecture and having a capital made up of volutes (spiral scrolls).
Istana	The Malay word for a palace.
jalousie	Literally, French for jealousy; a blind or shutter with fixed or moveable slats which slope upwards from the outside so as to exclude sun and rain but give shade, ventilation and visual privacy.
kampung, kampong	The Malay word for village.
lintel	A horizontal structural member spanning an opening which carries the weight above, usually of steel, masonry, concrete or timber.
lorong	The Malay word for a lane or small street.
louvre, louver	Mostly used in the plural to mean an arrangement of overlapping blades or slats, fixed or adjustable, designed to admit air but to exclude the sun and rain.
minaret	A tall, slender tower or turret in, or connected to, a mosque, with stairs leading up to one or more balconies from which the muezzin calls the faithful to prayer.
Neo-Classicism	The last phase of European Classicism of the late 18th and early 19th century characterised by monumentality, a sparing use of ornament and a strict use of the Orders of architecture.
Order	In Classical architecture, an Order signifies a column (with base, except in the Greek Doric, shaft and capital) together with the entablature which it supports. The Greek Orders were the Doric, Ionic and Corinthian and the Romans added the Tuscan and Composite.
pagoda	A temple or sacred building of the Orient, especially a tower, usually of pyramidal form, built over the relics of Buddha or a saint.
Palladio	A style of architecture strictly using Roman forms as set forth in the publications of Andrea Palladio (1518–1580), the Italian architect of Vicenza; the main revival was in England under the influence of Lord Burlington in the 18th century. Palladio actually imitated ancient Roman architecture without regard to Classical principles.
pediment	A term used in Classical architecture for the gable end of a building enclosed by the two sloping lines of a roof and supported by the entablature.
Peranakan	This is the name given to the Straits-born Chinese as distinct from the China-born Chinese. It is a Malay word made up from 'per' which is a prefix for 'to participate in the action of' and 'anan' (child) or anakan (to be born); literally, a person who was born here or a person of this place.

pier A mass of masonry as distinct from a column, from which an arch springs, in an arcade or bridge; also, a thickened section of a wall placed at intervals along its length to provide lateral support or to take concentrated vertical loads.

pilaster A rectangular or semi-circular pier or pillar, engaged with a wall and often with a base and capital in the form of one of the Orders of architecture.

pintu besar Pintu is the Malay word for door and besar means large, hence the main door.

pintu pagar Pagar is the Malay word for fence or hedge, hence, fence door; a half door placed in front of the main door to afford privacy but give ventilation when the main door is open.

plinth The lowest square member of the base of a column.

portico A colonnaded space forming an entrance or vestibule, with a roof supported on at least one side by columns.

Renaissance A French word applied to the 'rebirth' of Classical architecture all over Europe in the 15th and 16th centuries.

Rococo The term applied to a type of late Renaissance ornament characterised by rock-like forms, scrolls, shells; prevalent in France in the final phase of the Baroque period around the middle of the 18th century.

rustication A method of forming masonry with roughened surfaces and recessed joints; principally used in buildings of the Renaissance period.

Saracenic style This term is used to describe Muslim architecture or any features in it.

shophouse A shop with a dwelling above. Shophouses were usually built as part of a terrace, often with their upper floors overhanging the first storey to form a pedestrian covered arcade. They were characteristic of the 19th and early 20th century commercial centres of Southeast Asian towns and cities.

Straits Chinese Those Chinese who were born in the area of the Straits of Malacca, distinct from those who were China-born; also referred to as Peranakan. The men are called Babas and the women referred to as Nonyas.

streetscape A portion of a street which the eye can comprehend in a single view, including all the buildings and elements of which it consists.

Tudor style A style of architecture which was the final development of English Perpendicular Gothic architecture during the reigns of Henry VII and Henry VIII (1485–1547) preceding Elizabethan architecture.

Victorian style A style of architecture which was revivalist and eclectic and was produced in the 19th century in Great Britain and named after the reign of Queen Victoria (1837–1901).

villa A large elaborate dwelling with outbuildings and gardens of the Roman and Renaissance times; in modern times it refers to a detached urban or suburban house of a superior type and often with some pretension.